STOP
DIGGING!

To: The Dollar
Family

Continue to change the
world. May God bless and
keep you. I hope you sincerely
enjoy our series.

Be empowered!
Cliff ___ IV

Unless otherwise noted, all Scripture taken from the King James Version. Scripture noted as such taken from the Good News Translation – Second Edition, copyright © 1992 by American Bible Society. Used by permission. Scripture noted as such taken from Young's Literal Translation of the Holy Bible, copyright © 1898.

This publication contains the opinions and ideas of its author and is designed to provide useful information in regard to the subject matter covered. It is sold with the understanding that the publisher is not engaged in rendering legal, financial, tax preparation, or other professional services. Laws vary from state to state, and if the reader requires expert assistance or legal advice, a competent professional should be consulted. Readers should not rely on this (or any other) publication for financial guidance, but should do their own homework and make their own decisions. The author and publisher specifically disclaim any responsibility for any liability, loss, or risk, personal or otherwise, which is incurred as a consequence, directly or indirectly, of the use and application of any of the contents of this book.

Cover illustration by Emily Costa.
Cover and interior design by Pneuma Books, LLC.
For more information, visit www.pneumabooks.com

Publisher's Cataloging-in-Publication
(Provided by Quality Books, Inc.)

Goins, Cliff Tony.
  Stop digging! : a spiritual guide to financial
freedom and sound stewardship / by Cliff "Tony" Goins
IV. -- 1st ed.
  p. cm. -- (Adelphos Publishing's economic empowerment
series ; 1)
  LCCN 2002117792
  ISBN 0-9727418-0-1

  1. Finance, Personal--Religious aspects--
Christianity. 2. Christians--Finance, Personal.
I. Title. II. Title: Stop digging!

HG179.G645 2003   332.024
                   QBI03-200047

10 09 08 07 06 05 04 03   6 5 4 3 2 1

WHAT PEOPLE ARE SAYING ABOUT STOP DIGGING!

"Masterfully done! Superb! Cliff does a great job of exposing the root of financial insecurity and presenting spiritual solutions to solve money issues. Whether you make a five-, six-, or seven-figure income, you will love the advice this book offers."

—*Dr. John E. Guns, Senior Pastor,*
St. Paul Missionary Baptist Church, Jacksonville, FL

"Cliff's four Ps of preparation, prudence, partnership, and productivity are the qualities of nearly every successful money manager. What a great marriage of spirituality and personal finance!"

—*Eric T. McKissack, CFA, former Vice Chairman and*
Portfolio Manager, Ariel Capital Management, Inc.

"*Stop Digging!* and *Start Planting!* offer a rational, down-to-earth plan that combines spiritual development with financial responsibility, wealth creation and resource management. Goins and Thomas have done the hard work of identifying the common thread between personal financial development and spiritual actualization. Readers will enjoy the timely message of the series intended to provide a concrete roadmap for success in both the spiritual and secular life. Congratulations for providing a worthwhile tool for insuring the means to achieve the best life has to offer."

—*Michael Manns, Vice President and Senior Portfolio Manager,*
American Express Financial Advisors

"The financial services industry has taken great efforts to confuse the public. The confusion is now so great that people have been driven to indecision. It is refreshing to see a new commonsense approach to thinking about finance. Kudos to the authors of *Stop Digging!* and *Start Planting!*"

—*Lyle Logan, Senior Vice President, The Northern Trust Company*

"Inspiring and introspective! *Stop Digging!* provides invaluable advice that almost anyone can use." —*Carla Norfleet Taylor, CFA*

"*Stop Digging!* is a unique way of empowering you to do the right things to take care of yourself both spiritually and financially. Mixing faith and financial facts, Cliff effectively provides you with tools you need to manage your resources."

—*Donald G. McCoy, director-level human resources professional*

"Cliff goes beyond the mere top-ten-list approach of what to do with money to establish a spiritual base for all money decisions. The chapter on how God feels about partnerships was enlightening. I can't recall hearing that topic being dealt with before the way Cliff did. The end result is a work by a person who studies the Word. 'Somebody say, Amen!'"

—*Maurice L. Haywood, CFA, Vice President,*
Portfolio Manager/Analyst, Brown Capital Management Inc.

"God has definitely provided Cliff and Shundrawn with His grace. *Stop Digging!* and *Start Planting!* is light and easy reading that have deep and powerful messages. While the books are educational, they inspire and inform. This two-part series provides the key that will unlock the doors for financial and personal success for many. It is a wonderful resource that should be added to everyone's reading list."

—*Monique Bernoudy, Associate Athletics Director,*
Northern Illinois University

"The role of money in the Christian lifestyle can be a confusing subject, with people offering opinions that range from limited to self-serving. In *Stop Digging!* and *Start Planting!*, Ministers Thomas and Goins get it right. They provide for us a model for personal financial success through the application of impeccable educational and professional credentials, real world financial sector experience and perspectives that can only be described as anointed. They give readers a roadmap to personal wealth that is in lockstep with the Christian walk by keeping money in its proper place. They definitely show that we don't have to be 'of the world' in order to find fulfillment and success 'in the world'. I recommend this series of guides to everyone."

—*Darrell Williams, Chief Investment Officer,*
Telecommunications Development Fund

ADELPHOS

STOP
DIGGING!

A Spiritual Guide to Financial
Freedom and Sound Stewardship
CLIFF GOINS IV, CPA

Stop (verb) — to cease activity or operation; to come to an end (especially suddenly); to kill.

Digging (verb tense) — the act of hollowing out or forming a hole by removing.

Dedication

To the 95 percent of the world that dominates only 5 percent of the world's wealth and to all those who seek to discover, once and for all, the Truth about the often controversial subject of God, man, and mammon.

ACKNOWLEDGMENTS

First giving honor to the awesome gift of the Holy Spirit that enables me to communicate with the Father and opens up my understanding of His inexhaustible Word. All praises due to my Lord and Savior, Jesus Christ, for without Him I can do nothing. I would be remiss if I did not spend some time thanking some of the wonderful folks that were instrumental in bringing this project to fruition.

Special thanks to my virtuous wife, Janelle, who has tolerated my shenanigans throughout this entire process. Mere words cannot express the love I have for you!

Thank you to my brother, cousin, friend and business partner Shundrawn A. Thomas, his lovely wife, Latania, and precious son, Javon. Now is the acceptable time.

Thanks to my dad, Clifton III, my mom, Reneè and my sweet, sweet "baby" sisters (smile) Cherrice, Alisha, and Michelle.

Thank you to the Goins family at large (there are too many of you all to name); the Frazier family at large (ditto); my pastors, Gary and Audrey Thomas; my faithful *Live Heaven on Earth* readers (keep growing); my Florida A & M University folks; my Minne-SNOW-ta crew (Minnesota rocks! — smile); my Kellogg friends (especially classes of 2000, 2001, and 2002); Lou Holland and all of the great people at Holland Capital Management, L.P.; the distinguished men of Alpha Phi Alpha Fraternity, Inc. (especially the Beta Nu and Mu chapters); the Anubisinians; the fellas — Chris, Ivor, Dave, Jermaine, Travis and Rahman — our relationships have ebbed and flowed on many levels, but know that I love you and pray God's favor over each one of your lives; the Sumner family; the Elzy family (and extended); the Marshall family (Brian, Rhonda, Adonijah, Ariana, and Alexander); the Johnson family (especially Sally, Sidney, and Elonda); and Look Up & Live Full Gospel Church and Evangelistic Crusaders COGIC in Chicago.

I also must recognize a group of people that probably do not know the influence they have had on this project: Pastor Carlton Arthurs; Dr. Dana Carson; Pastor John E. Guns; Dr. Creflo A. Dollar; Bishop T. D. Jakes; Pastor Bill Winston; Bishop Paul S. Morton. Sr.; Dr. Joyce Meyer; Fred Hammond; Eric McKissack; Jim Reynolds; Lyle Logan; Professor Steven Rogers (and his charming wife, Michele); Stuart A. Tayor II; Ed Bachrach; Steve Kumagai; Diane Lyngstad; Julie Morton; Kathy Quandt; Terri Tremmel; Debbie Russell; Russell Martin; Monique Bernoudy; Mike Manns; Donald McCoy; Dawn Crowder; and Venita Fields.

This book was inspired by the genius of the late Juanita Goins, the late Mother Maimie Till Mobley, Mother Annie Goodman, the late Dr. Martin Luther King, Jr., Dr. Myles Munroe, Pastor John Cherry, Walter W. Whitman, Jr., Pastor Derrick Jackson, the late Pastor George Liggins, Pastors Gary and Audrey Thomas, and Minister Shundrawn Thomas.

Lastly, I must thank our book editing and design team at Pneuma Books (www.pneumabooks.com) and our website gurus at Liquid Soul Media (www.LiquidSoulMedia.com) and Diamond Lounge Creative (www.diamondloungecreative.com). Is everyone ready for the next project?

CONTENTS

Part III   *Getting My Soil Ready:*
         The Four P's to Reestablishing a Strong
         Financial Foundation

Part IV   *Appendices*

FOREWORD

Who Am I?

I'm just an ordinary guy. I'm not a celebrity or even famous for that matter. Well, not yet anyway! I guess that begs the question, why am I writing this foreword? After all, conventional wisdom dictates that a foreword written by a famous person provides a book with greater credibility. Fortunately, I am not burdened with the task of rendering this book credible because its teachings are truly extraordinary. As a child of God, I believe that the answers to everyday problems are found in God's Word. However, my faith falls short at times when it comes to dealing with money. I'm not afraid to admit that money is important to me. Since we are important to God, and He knew money would be important to us, He made certain to deal with the money resource in His Word. How many people know that we need revelation knowledge to understand the truths that are found in God's Word? How many people know we have to seek truth to find it? I know that God wants me to be a good steward and enjoy the prosperity that only comes from serving Him. I also know that I must seek the truth through His Word, and I want to learn from one of His most gifted servants. I am reading this book because God has a revelation for me concerning the money resource.

Who Are You?

You are probably a little like me. First of all, I know money is important to you. That's why you picked up this book! Other people know you care about money too. You likely picked up this book because you want to learn more about being a good steward. Moreover, you are concerned about what God has to say about sound stewardship. If you are like me, you have had money problems in your past or you may be experiencing them in the present. You may be looking to right financial missteps of yesteryear or simply trying to avoid past mistakes. Most importantly, you care about having the proper relationship with God. You understand that putting money in the proper perspective is paramount to establishing the right relationship with God. You want to learn how God expects you to approach the money resource as well as have dominion in your personal finances. You want to free yourself from worry and anxiety related to money so you can be all that God has purposed you to be. Financial soundness and soundness of mind are simply the fruit produced by the proper application of God's Word. True financial freedom is achieved when we scrap our plan and adhere to God's plan.

Who Is Cliff "Tony" Goins IV?

Aside from being a man of many names, Cliff is an ordinary individual just like us. However, Cliff has an extraordinary gift. God has given Cliff the ability to draw fresh insights from His Word in many areas, including economic empowerment. God has given him an awesome revelation concerning the money resource and achieving financial freedom. Cliff is a lover and not a fighter. By that I mean he loves God's Word and he loves God's people. Rather than fight against the truth found in God's Word, he embraces it. He uses his gifts to preach and teach these truths to others. Cliff's thoughts are truly groundbreaking. He breaks up the fallow ground of years of bondage and nonproductivity and releases believers with the freedom that can only be found through the revelation of God's Word. Cliff is a devoted husband, son, brother, and one of God's lights in the world. Cliff is also a true friend, and I am blessed to call him a friend of mine. In his book *Stop Digging!*, Cliff lays a spiritual foundation that empowers the believer to achieve financial freedom. As we literally turn the pages of life we learn the proper relationship between God, man, and mammon; we learn the role of mankind in the earth; we learn the role of money in the earth; and we learn the keys to being productive with the money resource. May you be as empowered as I was as you embrace part one of Adelphos Publishing's *Economic Empowerment Series, Stop Digging!*

Faithfully Yours,
Shundrawn A. Thomas
Author, *Start Planting! A Spiritual Guide to Wealth Creation and Successful Investing*

PREFACE

The Digger Mentality

As a certified public accountant with an MBA and extensive financial services industry experience, I hope to bring to you a practical perspective on the believer's quest for financial freedom. As God's child and a minister to the people of God, I hope to impart the revelation of God's Word given to me by the Holy Spirit concerning the relationship involving God, man, and mammon.

Nowadays, men and women write numerous volumes on *How to Get Debt-free in Seven Days!*, *Financial Freedom for Morons*, and the like, but few authors seem to adequately address the root of financial instability. The root of financial instability is this: We, as a people, have cultivated countless generations of diggers.

We live in a culture predicated on consumption — acquiring as much as possible as soon as possible. This pattern represents a destructive digger mentality. This book was written to discuss the concept of digging; to show there is absolutely no scriptural basis for digging; and to free God's people from digging.

Eccl. 10:8 says, "He that diggeth a pit shall fall into it; and whoso breaketh an hedge, a serpent shall bite him." This verse provides a foundational scripture for this project and brings home two points. First, if you dig, you will fall. This will happen 100 percent of the time. Second, when you forsake your Hedge, you will be bitten. This will also happen 100 percent of the time.

Digger behavior begins in the mind. Ask yourself: What do I think about the most? This book provides a new perspective on financial freedom and will go a long way in transforming the digger mentality into one of productivity. This is book one of an economic empowerment series and is crucial to establishing a foundation for economic freedom and growth. This is not your run-of-the-mill, seven-steps, self-help book series. This series is all about self-enlightenment and destroying the do-it-yourself mentality.

The first step in destroying the digger mentality is to believe God's system is the most efficient and effective one. The second step is to make the quality choice to operate according to His system. If you really think about it, this is a book that should never have been written. This book is a powerful reminder of several truths.

- We were originally created to be the sons of God and we were blessed by God with every resource necessary to be successful and to prosper.
- God has a specific operating order and He designed us to operate just like Him.
- God did not want to create generations of robots so He empowered us with the power of choice. God knows true love comes out of the power of choice.
- There are only three steps to reaching financial freedom or any other kind of freedom:
  - Building the proper attitude: Think like God thinks.
  - Using God's words: Speak like God speaks.
  - Implementing proper behaviors: Act like God acts.

Digging causes the majority of God's people to struggle financially, mentally, spiritually and physically. Digging is caused by lack of knowledge and lack of understanding. I pray the Holy Spirit will open up your understanding so you can experience and achieve all that God has prepared for you in this earth realm.

My Stop Digging! Start Planting! Testimony

Upon deciding to pursue a graduate business degree and observing the high cost of attending business school full-time, I realized that I was not financially prepared to make the transition. I had spent all of my time since undergraduate school working diligently in corporate America. All I had to show for it, however, was a bunch of CDs (compact discs not certificates of deposit) and a nice fat car note with high insurance to boot. I also had some pocket change parked in mutual funds and the 3 percent per pay period (plus the company match) that I was dumping into my 401(k) plan. In spite of my job in financial services and my collection of personal finance books, I was far from financially free. What was clear was that I would have to borrow a nice sum of money from somewhere to return to school.

Even with my then sporadic commitment to Christ and questionable behavior, God blessed me to be accepted by every program that I applied to. In my mind, I ideally wanted to be back in Chicago near its strong financial community, but I was open to opportunities elsewhere. My first acceptance letter came from University A and included a full, tuition-only scholarship. Yee-haw! Now all I have to do is borrow money for housing. Letter number two rolled in from University B with a very reasonable partial scholarship. I really liked my visit there and the people were fantastic. Letter three came from the campus of University C — where the people were also terrific — coupled with a partial scholarship that paled in comparison to the previous two. Lastly, after much hope and much discussion, I was accepted at University D with a scholarship equal to that at University C. Let's recap. I have close to no money in my bank account, a full-tuition scholarship, a nice partial-tuition scholarship, and two decent partial-tuition scholarships on the table. What's a guy to do? From my school visits, Universities B and C were tops on my list, but there was still the outstanding money question.

I crafted a plan to attempt to negotiate higher scholarships using the University A deal as leverage. The plan worked great at Universities B and D, but University C would not budge. Something inside of me exclaimed, "You need to move back to Chicago!" All I could think about was the fact that I really wanted to go to University C, but it would force me to borrow the most money. University D did offer more money, but they were still ranked behind both B and C on my list. There's that voice again: Don't worry about the money. What's a guy to do? I trusted that voice and decided to move back to Chicago to attend University C — Northwestern. To save a little money, I would move in with my family and make the hour or so commute to Evanston...every...single...day.

Back in the Windy City, God dealt with me about changing my sinful ways and returning to Him. I was inclined to attend Look Up and Live Full Gospel Church, pastored by the father of my long-time friend, Shundrawn. Little did I know, I was in for a radical change. I began attending church regularly. After a while, the Spirit led me to attend Bible study regularly. (In all my life in church, I don't think I had ever been to a Bible study). God began to strip me piece-by-piece of the awful habits and attitudes I had picked up over the previous twelve years. Then it happened. In the fall of 2000, I was finally able to overcome a temptation that had me in serious bondage and unable to achieve my purpose in this life. The digger mentality had finally left the building. Later that year, I received a word from God saying, "You have been running and running and running. It is time for you to stop. I want to use you while you are young." Wow.

Why is God always so vague about these things? What's a guy to do? I prayed and studied and prayed and studied and prayed some more.

God began to show me my education and career in financial services. He began to show me my desire to see people financially free. He increased my burden for the deliverance of the body of Christ from the money hang-up. Next, the Spirit led me to begin a weekly e-mail ministry called Live Heaven on Earth. It became a weekly Bible study for my readers where I break down different topics as the Spirit leads. I began to hone my writing skills. I began to craft my unique writing style. Simultaneously, I began to teach an economic empowerment series at church that attempted to connect the Word of God with personal finance principles. At the same time, I, along with several of my classmates, worked on a business plan designed to address the dearth of financial knowledge in the church market. Some wheels were in motion, but for what? Then came a conversation that took place when Shundrawn returned from vacation in Spain at the end of the summer of 2001. Here is my two-second version.

Shundrawn: "I think I'm going to write a book."

Me: "That's great!"

Shundrawn: "No. You don't understand. I need you to write it with me. I was scribbling some notes on a pad in the hotel in Spain that I want to share with you. I already have the titles: *Stop Digging!* and *Start Planting!* I want to do a series."

Me: "What are you thinking?"

Shundrawn: "You know how we have been talking about economic empowerment and being able to spread that word in the unique way God has given it to us? Well, what better way to do that than with books. You can use what God has given you concerning stewardship and I will use what He is giving me concerning investing. What do you think? Are you interested?"

Me: "Sign me up!"

Since this conversation, meticulous work has been done to bring you a fresh look at God's perspective on money. This fresh look is one that I can finally embrace and I hope you learn to embrace it too. Now I realize that the voice I heard was the Spirit of God trying to influence me to get me in the right position so that God could bless me and bless you through me. God is the Maker of all resources so He told me: Don't worry about the money. Since returning to Chicago, God has transformed my thinking, revealed some of my gifts to me, presented me with a gorgeous and loving wife, and freed me from the digger mentality. These four things alone have resulted and will continue to result in financial increase beyond my imagination.

Out of Place, Out of Peace

How God Created Me to Prosper

Starting Point

Let us establish some working definitions to assist us in our study.

- ❧ God is the Father and Creator of all things visible and invisible (Col. 1:9-19).
- ❧ The name Jesus means God is salvation. The title Christ refers to the Anointed One of God and His Anointing.
- ❧ Jesus the Christ or Christ Jesus was the Word of God made flesh and is the Son of God (John 1). The Word of God can also be substituted as the word *Wisdom*.
- ❧ The word *blessed* means endowed and/or empowered by God.
- ❧ The word *son* is the Greek word *huios* (hwee-os') and signifies the relationship of offspring to parent (i.e., it does not designate gender).
- ❧ The word *man* in the Bible generally refers to all of mankind, but must be read contextually to determine its proper use.
- ❧ The Anointing is the awesome power of the Holy Spirit working in and on the behalf of the sons offspring of God.

These definitions will help us read the Bible with understanding.

In the Beginning...

Gen. 1:1 "In the beginning God created (brought into existence something new) the heaven and the earth."

John 1:1, 3, 14 "In the beginning was the Word, and the Word was with God, and the Word was God...All things were made (put together) by him (the Word); and without him was not any thing made that was made...And the Word was made flesh (Jesus Christ), and dwelt among us...full of grace and truth."

These verses are frequently quoted, but seldom understood. Through the magnificence of the preparation of the earth for inhabitation by mankind (Genesis 1), we see the uncompromising order of God: God thinks; God speaks His Word; The Spirit of God moves. This helps us understand John when he states in 1 John 5:7, "For there are three that bear record in heaven, the Father, the Word, and the Holy Ghost: and these three are one." You see there is no way to separate God from His Word or the results of His Word, which are enabled by the Holy Spirit.

Now, I'm sure you're thinking, "What does this have to do with me? I thought this book was going to help me with my finances!" Good news! This book will not only help you with your finances, but it will enhance the quality of your life.

Original Agreement

Gen. 1:26, 27-28 "And God said (spoke the Word), Let us make man in our image (a reproduction or imitation), after our likeness (nature)...So God created man in his [own] image, in the image of God created he him; male and female created he them. And God blessed (empowered) them, and God said unto them, Be fruitful, and multiply, and replenish the earth, and subdue it: have dominion over the fish of the sea, and over the fowl of the air, and over every living thing that moveth upon the earth."

What happened here? First, this is not the formation of the physical man, Adam, in the earth. This is the creation of all mankind in the spirit realm. God is a Spirit (John 4:24). God created man as a spirit (see verses above). Secondly, mankind just received its destiny or purpose for existence. That purpose is to be God's representative, steward, or agent in the earth, to have fellowship with Him, and to operate just like He operates. We can think of it as a career. Let's look further at the aspects of the original agreement.

Career Description

Here's mankind's original career description: produce, increase, replenish, subdue. Everything in mankind's career description is an action verb. Moreover, everything in the career description requires work. Lastly, each task given to mankind by God requires planting (more on that in part two of this series), not digging.

Operation Manual

Notice mankind was designed to operate just like God. Let us go through God's order of operation. First, think the Word. Then, speak the Word. Finally, the Holy Spirit facilitates what is spoken.

God's Management Style

God believes in employee empowerment and entrepreneurship. He gave mankind complete control over all resources in the earth realm. God furnished mankind with the ultimate in economic empowerment.

The Adams Family

The name Adam refers to mankind. In fact, when we read Gen. 5:1-2, we find Adam is referred to in the plural form ("...and called *their* name Adam..."). This is not hard to comprehend since we just established that all of mankind was created at one time in the spirit.

> *Gen. 2:7* "And the Lord God formed man [of] the dust of the ground, and breathed into his nostrils the breath of life; and man became a living soul."

Here we see the spirit of Adam or mankind being transported into the natural realm by God. The word *became* is the past tense of the word *become*, which means to pass from one state to another. So the spirit man passed from the spirit realm (invisible) into the natural realm (visible). In Gen. 2:1, we find "the heavens and earth were finished, and all the host of them." As the story in Genesis 1 and 2 unfolds, we find only one thing was declared "not good" — the original physical male man, Adam, being alone. At that point, God brought all of the creatures and animals He had shaped out of the ground to Adam to be named and to see if Adam could find a helpmeet. While Adam successfully named the animals, he found no suitable creature to fulfill the role of a helpmeet. Therefore, he did not choose one. However, God knew that He had already placed Adam's helpmeet in him. Understand that God created everything in the earth realm to produce after its own kind (Genesis 1). When it came time to make another physical man, He took that new man (female) out of the original physical male man (Gen. 2:21-25). Upon laying eyes on the woman, Adam knew he had found a helpmeet.

Now everything is good. The Adams family is finally ready to take on the world!

Breach of Agreement

In Genesis 3, the fellowship arrangement takes a turn for the worse. It turns out that with all this responsibility and control, the Adams thought they could figure out how to operate in the earth realm independent of God's instructions. They convinced themselves to stop thinking according to the orders they had received from the Father, or Source, of their existence. They simply stopped thinking like God. This disobedience to the One who fathered them and empowered them ushered into existence a contract breach that adversely affected everything in the earth. As a result, all seeds that would come out of the creatures and plants in the earth were doomed as well. We, as the seeds of Adam, share in the misfortune they caused. This misfortune manifests itself in death or lack of fellowship with God (read: lack of fellowship or relationship). Instead of planting or sowing into the earth, the Adams decided to take from the earth. *This is what created generations of diggers.*

Reinstatement of Agreement

However, we find in Gen. 3:15 God in His infinite wisdom knew His greatest supernatural creation would overestimate his God-given natural ability. Consequently, God had already devised a plan to redeem His man from his own evil ways. (God knows the ending of all things so he plans the beginning accordingly). Therefore, He planned to send the Word (the original maker of mankind — John 1:3) to restore life to mankind and to place him in his rightful place as God's express image in the earth. For this, the Word of God came to earth in the form of Jesus Christ. Jesus died as the sacrifice for man's transgressions and was resurrected to conquer the penalty for man's disobedience, which is death or separation from God. This sacrifice paved the way for man to be reestablished as holy and to be able to receive the gift of the Holy Spirit. If you read Genesis 1-3 closely, you will find what man ultimately lost through his and her disobedience was holiness — God's standard and the only way to cultivate a relationship with Him.

The whole purpose for the sacrifice of Jesus Christ is to restore mankind back to the relationship God intended us to have with Him when He came up with the "man" concept in the first place. That is why men and women need to be saved. We need to be delivered from the mindset of digging. The mindset of digging leads to death, which is separation from God forever. Digging can be perceived in many areas of life. However, we will discover that all manifestations of digging eventually come back to money.

Understanding Mankind's Purpose

Let us revisit the purpose of Adam. When we study the name *Adam* further, we find it literally means earth. When we read the Bible, we learn God takes the idea of naming a person very seriously. On numerous occasions, He told people exactly what to name their offspring. Why on earth would He do this?

Your name is what gives you identity, purpose, and inheritance. So we find God named mankind *Earth*, which suggests our identification, reason for existence, and life's legacy is all tied to the earth realm. The second thing to observe is that in Gen. 1:28, God equipped mankind with everything we would ever need to be successful or prosperous in the earth. When He "blessed them" He was essentially giving mankind all the power and ability needed to reach our destiny or to fulfill our purpose. The last thing to note is man's legacy is directly related to God's instructions — be fruitful, multiply, replenish the earth, and subdue the earth, which leads to domination. So what exactly does all that mean?

1. Be Fruitful — This is the concept of productivity, which is

discussed in detail in chapter 10. Specifically, this is a call to be productive in the plan and purpose of God.

2. Multiply — This is the concept of increase. Everything in the earth realm reaches out for more and more. God set a spiritual principle of increase in the earth realm. It is akin to the fact that God is a God that can never run out of any resource. Think abundant wealth!

3. Replenish the Earth — This is the concept of perfection or excellence. God does not want His people to lack anything so He says, "Make sure the earth is fully supplied."

4. Subdue the Earth — This is the concept of order. God is a God of order and all things must be done decently and in order.

5. Domination — This is the concept of leadership or influence. God has given us the decision-making power and the ability to change any situation in the earth realm by implementing the aforementioned mandates.

Mankind's legacy is this: Everything man touches is supposed to be prosperous. The word *prosper* means favorable; marked by success; enjoying vigorous and healthy growth. God created man to be productive, to increase, to be complete, to be in control — to exercise dominance in the earth realm. He identified us as *Earth.* He told us our purpose as it relates to the earth. Our inheritance is prosperity and peace in the earth. The sole reason man is in the earth is to share in and experience the abundance and peace of God.

As we compare that awesome purpose and inheritance to our current financial situation, do we see a disconnect? What is the source of the disconnect? The source brings us back to the difference between digging and planting. Productivity, increase, maturity, order, and leadership all have one common theme — planting. What do we mean by that? Planting represents a foundational action for growth to occur (Shundrawn Thomas covers this in detail in part two of this series). Each of the instructions laid out by God and, in fact, the very way God prepared the earth was established on the spiritual principle of sowing (planting) and reaping. So let us better understand the process using a simple example.

Imagine you want an apple tree and God has given you one apple seed. You now must decide what to do with the apple seed. Now, you are pretty smart so you know all you have to do is plant that puppy in the ground, give it some TLC, and soon you will get your apple tree. Several weeks pass and you run out of the house, but there is nothing there except that same wet patch of dirt. A few months pass and much to your dismay that same mud patch is still there. You think to yourself, "This must not be working." So what do you do? You go to the garage and grab your shovel. You are going to get to the bottom of this! Literally! You dig up the seed only to find germination was taking place and you have now ruined the process. You have destroyed the foundation for growth. No apples for you!

This, my friends, is how we treat the money seed. We do entirely too much digging and not enough planting. We lack patience and do not exercise good judgment when making financial decisions. We are constantly led by how we feel or what we deserve as opposed to being led by the spiritual principle of good stewardship. We are operating outside of the purpose or will of God.

The World Is Mine?

Ps. 24:1 "The earth [is] the Lord's, and the fulness thereof; the world, and they that dwell therein."

Ps. 50:12 "If I (God) were hungry, I would not tell thee: for the world [is] mine, and the fulness thereof."

This earth and all that is in it does not belong to mankind. The earth has been prepared for mankind's habitation, but it is the property of God. This is a sticking point for many of us. My house! My job! My kids! My money! My wife! My husband! My life! My! My! My! My! My! My! My! Newsflash: None of it is yours. Let us deal with a few of the "Mys".

My kids

Ps. 127:3 "Lo, children [are] an heritage of the Lord: [and] the fruit of the womb [is his] reward."

My money

Deut. 8:18 "But thou shalt remember the Lord thy God: for [it is] he that giveth thee the power to get wealth..."

My wife

Prov. 19:14 "Houses and riches [are] the inheritance of fathers: and a prudent wife [is] from the Lord."

My life

Gen. 2:7 "And the Lord God formed man [of] the dust of the ground, and breathed into his nostrils the breath of life; and man became a living soul."

Sounds to me like all things, your very life included, belong to God! Now that we understand all elements of this earthly life are God's property, we need to understand our particular role in the earth. That role is one of stewardship.

The Revelation of Stewardship

The word *steward* denotes one employed to manage the domestic concerns of another; a fiscal agent for another; one who actively directs affairs of another. Did anybody notice the word *another* in all of the previous definitions? *Another* means some other. Or we can plainly say, "Not you!" A steward is an active, fiscally responsible manager of someone else's property. *Active* signifies functioning and productive. *Fiscally responsible* deliberately relates to money! Accordingly, mankind has been given custody of God's money, which is the earth itself.

"Mr. Author, you are losing me. The earth is not money!" Of course it is. Where do you live? Does it cost money to live there? Where do you work? Do they pay you? Does it cost money to get there? Does it cost money for the business to even be in that location? Where do you worship? Does your ministry operate rent-free? Where do you vacation? Do you just get up and go without grabbing some money? I can only give you what the Holy Spirit gave me. We need only go back to Genesis 2 to check out the first piece of property man had to manage. Pastor Derrick Jackson of the Wheaton Christian Center pointed out this scripture at a conference I recently attended.

> *Gen. 2:10-12* "And a river went out of Eden to water the garden; and from thence it was parted, and became into four heads. The name of the first [is] Pison: that [is] it which compasseth the whole land of Havilah, where [there is] gold; And the gold of that land [is] good: there [is] bdellium and the onyx stone."

Do we need any commentary? Bdellium is similar to myrrh. Many of you biblical scholars will recall the wise men (there were likely more than three) presented the child Jesus with myrrh along with gold and frankincense. "You mean they presented Jesus with money?" And the church said, "Yes!" It is not different than what God presented man with: the earth, which in the ultimate sense is representative of God's wealth. We need to stop perpetuating the myth that Jesus was poor and Christians should be poor for Christ's sake. We need to read the passage of scripture in 2 Corinthians 8, which is the source of that myth, in its proper context. Paul was ministering to a specific assembly on the importance of giving of their substance in a natural and spiritual sense (i.e., not hoarding). The earth is a place of abundance and God put mankind here to be the steward of everything it has to offer.

When we tie stewardship back to the notion of digging, we discover the adjectives *functioning* and *productive* are the polar opposite of digging. Digging in its essence implies the concept of subtraction. There is nothing functional or productive about subtracting from the earth. Therefore, as a digger, one is by definition not a steward. If we do not function as a steward, we are out of God's divine order. We were created to be stewards. If we find ourselves drowning in debt, we are not being good stewards. If we spend more than we make, we are not being good stewards. If we don't even know how much money we spend in a given month, we are not being good stewards. Thank God there is time to learn how to be a proper steward. Join me as we learn to *Stop Digging!* It is the first step toward operating in the prosperous environment God created us to live in.

Stop Digging!

SEEDS FOR YOUR SOIL

The Word of God: John 1:1-14

1. In verses 1 through 5, what do we learn about the Word of God? What does that tell us about the origin of life and money?

2. In verses 6 through 13, what do we learn about the Light? What does this passage tell us about the purpose of the Light and the origin of mankind?

3. In verse 14, what is the Word full of and why is that important for the believer to truly experience financial freedom?

Restoration of the Earth and Mankind's Assignment of Stewardship: Genesis 1 and 2

1. What did God create first (hint: the answer is in John 1:1)? Why is this important to the believer?

2. What did God say about mankind when He created them? Why is this important to the believer?

3. What resources did God supply mankind with and what charge did He give them?

4. List the sequence of events in Genesis 2. Think about how it relates to your relationship with God, your relationship with other people, and your relationship with your finances.

Disobedience, the First and Only Sin: Genesis 3

1. What went wrong here? How is that related to what can go wrong in your financial life?

2. What was the result of disobedience? How is that related to the believer?

God's Earth, Not Mine: Psalm 24 and Psalm 19

1. Who is the King of glory?

2. How should we approach the King of glory and His resources?

PART I

PUTTING THE DIRT BACK IN THE HOLE

Understanding the Money Resource

CHAPTER 1

I'm an Original

Why God Wants Me to Start Where I Am

Understanding the Value of Who You Are

What do most people in the world value most? Need a hint? What is this book about? That's right! Money! Now if you will recall a few pages ago, we found out that the earth is money. Well, what did God give to mankind? Watch how this thing works.

> *Ps. 8:4-6* "What is man, that thou art mindful of him? and the son of man, that thou visitest him? For thou hast made him a little lower than the angels, and hast crowned him with glory and honour. Thou madest him to have dominion over the works of thy hands; thou hast put all things under his feet."

Mindful and Visits

How many people know what it means to be mindful? It means God's thoughts are continually toward mankind. Another way to express that is to say: God's mind is full of you! Not only that, but

we have the gift of the Spirit of God living in us when we are baptized in the Spirit. Therefore, God is permanently visiting his man
by His Spirit. When we are born again, the lines of communication are open again. All we need to do is look within and stop looking in the sky.

Lower than the Angels?

Paul said something in his first letter to Corinth that completely
wrecked my comprehension of this phrase. 1 Cor. 6:3 reads, "Know
ye not that we shall judge angels? how much more things that per-
tain to this life?" We also find many instances in the Bible where the
angels actually serve mankind (Heb. 1:14, Exod. 23:20-22, Ps. 91:11-
12 to name a few). So the question is, why did God make us "lower
than the angels?" The simple answer is He actually did not make us
lower than the angels. The Hebrew word for what translators in-
terpreted as *angels* is the word *elohiym* (el-o-heem'). Anybody want
to guess what that term *elohiym* refers to? It specifically refers to the
supreme God. If we read chapter 1 of this book closely, that definition does not surprise us. God made us "a little lower" than Himself, not the angels!

Dominion

There is that word again. What is the purpose of man? Dominate in
the natural earth. Operate in an environment that radiates abundance of valuable material possessions or resources.

So what is the value of a man? God thinks so much of man He literally gives man all of His valuable material possessions to dominate,
enjoy, and manage. He gives man the opportunity and ability to make
decisions, to be creative, and to develop in an atmosphere of abundance. In other words, all of the spiritual and natural "money" of God
is at man's disposal. The ball is in our court.

Diversity and Intricacy

Since mankind was created to operate in a prosperous setting, let's figure out how to get back to the point of prosperity in our individual lives. The diversity of God is an awesome testament to His sovereignty. We must realize that God does not make duplicates. There is not one other person on this planet who can be you. David grasped that concept when he wrote Ps. 19:1-3: "The heavens declare the glory of God; and the firmament sheweth his handiwork. Day unto day uttereth speech, and night unto night sheweth knowledge. [There is] no speech nor language, [where] their voice is not heard."

He was essentially saying that all you have to do is open your eyes and look around you to witness the diversity and intricacy of God. To me the more interesting observation (and the one that is most relevant for mankind today) is the fact that everything God made is unique and designed for a specific purpose. Consider this: every person, barring unfortunate circumstances, possesses a pair of hands and a pair of feet. How many people believe hands should not be used as feet and vice-versa? Hands were made specifically to handle things whereas feet were made to move us from place to place. If we decided to use our hands to walk around, my sneaking suspicion is we would have an extremely difficult time trying to function properly.

If we do not use the things God has created for their specific purpose, they cannot work properly and consequently will not fulfill that specified purpose. Since mankind was created to operate in a prosperous environment, every day spent living in poverty, living from check to check, or living below God's standards, is a day of functioning improperly and experiencing lack of fulfillment deep down on the inside.

Fingers, Eyes, Teeth, and Molecules

When I asked God how to convey the concept of originality to His people, He showed me all of the developments of science as it relates to mankind. The dictionary defines *science* as the state of knowing — knowledge as distinguished from ignorance or misunderstanding. My pastor came up with a more accurate definition: science is mankind discovering (or coming into the knowledge of) what God already did when He created everything. With that in mind, scientists have "discovered" various ways to identify specific individuals — the fingers, the eyes, the teeth, and the DNA. Let us spend some time understanding the merits of these particular identification methods.

Fingers[A]

There are two important facts about fingerprints. One, fingerprints remain unchanged over an individual's lifetime. Fingerprints form in the womb at around five months and remain constant even after death. Two, all fingerprints are unique. No one has ever found identical prints and there are at least 64 billion fingerprint combinations possible, which is ten times the number of people on the earth. From this discovery, man eventually created classes of fingerprints according to common characteristics. However, this proved to be insufficient to actually identify a person. Consequently, scientists rely on small details to determine authentication or identification.

Eyes[B]

The iris is the colored ring that surrounds the pupil of the eye. Like the fingerprint, the iris remains stable and unchanged throughout life and each iris is absolutely individual. Additionally, the iris is the most personally distinct feature of the human body. No two irises are alike in their mathematical detail, even among identical twins; the iris has at least 244 independent characteristics to base comparisons. Similarly, the retina is a thin nerve (one-fiftieth of an inch) on the back of the eye that senses light and transmits impulses through the optic nerve to the brain. Again, the patterns of the blood vessels in the retina remain relatively stable throughout one's lifetime and are distinctive from person to person.

Teeth[C]

Forensic odontology is the identification discipline based upon the recognition of distinguishing features present in each person's dental structures. Odontology plays a major role in man-made and natural disasters. Teeth and dental restorations are the strongest parts of the human body and survive the power of fire and other destructive elements. Even a single dental radiograph can yield multiple points of comparison given that each tooth has a top and four sides.

Molecules[D]

Deoxyribonucleic acid (DNA) is a chemical code specifying a person's function, appearance, and lineage. It is described as the molecule of life and is unique in all individuals except identical twins. The DNA molecule is vast, is found in most cells of the body, and can be detected in bodily fluids. The structure of DNA allows it to repair and replicate itself. DNA is the template for the reproduction of genetic material and cellular information.

What can we take away from all of that wonderful scientific jargon? God does not make mistakes and your birth did not just happen. Nobody can be you! You are an original. No one thinks exactly like you. No one's hands, eyes, or teeth are exactly like yours. Unless you are an identical twin, no one's DNA is exactly like yours.

What Does God Say about Me Being Original?

Again, David was a man who realized the magnificence of God as the supreme authority over all heaven and earth. Let us go to the scriptures.

Ps. 138:8 "The Lord will perfect [that which] concerneth me: thy mercy, O Lord, [endureth] for ever: forsake not the works of thine own hands."

Ps. 139:1-3 "O Lord, thou hast searched me, and known [me]. Thou knowest my downsitting and mine uprising, thou understandest my thought afar off. Thou compassest my path and my lying down, and art acquainted [with] all my ways."

Ps. 139:5-8 "Thou hast beset me behind and before, and laid thine hand upon me. [Such] knowledge [is] too wonderful for me; it is high, I cannot [attain] unto it. Whither shall I go from thy spirit? or whither shall I flee from thy presence? If I ascend up into heaven, thou [art] there: if I make my bed in hell, behold, thou [art there]."

Ps. 139:13-16 "For thou hast possessed my reins: thou hast covered me in my mother's womb. I will praise thee; for I am fearfully [and] wonderfully made: marvellous [are] thy works; and [that] my soul knoweth right well. My substance was not hid from thee, when I was made in secret, [and] curiously wrought in the lowest parts of the earth. Thine eyes did see my substance, yet being unperfect; and in thy book all [my members] were written, [which] in continuance were fashioned, when [as yet there was] none of them."

Let us see if we can catch all of this. In Ps. 138:8, we see God is committed to perfecting those individual matters that exclusively concern us. This is personal! In Ps. 139:1-3, we find God has an intricate understanding of everything about us. In Ps. 139:5-8, we notice God is much more knowledgeable than we are. He knows where everything He has created is at all times. In Ps. 139:13-16, the teaching gets really rich. *Reins* is the Hebrew word *kilyah* (kil-yaw'), which refers to the human mind. *Possessed* in this context is the Hebrew word *qanah* (kaw-naw') — to create. So David is saying: You created my mind, or personality, and protected me in my mother's womb. *Fearfully* is the Hebrew word *yare* (yaw-ray'). *Yare* speaks of being in awe of or a state of reverence. Have you ever heard someone say, "I'm scared of you?" What they are saying is the thing you have done is so awesome I cannot even see myself doing it. *Wonderfully*, as it relates to this passage is *palah* (paw-law') in the Hebrew and literally means put a difference in or set apart. The phrase "curiously wrought" comes from the Hebrew word *raqam* (raw-kam') meaning to embroider. The word *substance* takes on two different meanings. In "My *substance* was not hid...", it is the Hebrew word *otsem* (o'-tsem) — power or strength. In other words, David is saying: You knew exactly what You were doing when You specifically made me the way You decided to. As it relates to "Thine eyes did see my *substance*...", substance is translated as the Hebrew word *golem* (go'-lem), which is a wrapped and unformed mass. The verse goes on to state that even in this covered and embryonic state God had already written the book on you. In layman's terms, God has a specific purpose for you according the talents and abilities He placed in you.

Before Ordained

We will explore the concept of "before ordained" through several scriptures. *Before* means in advance. *Ordained* means to establish by decree or law; to destine. What we need to comprehend, accept, and believe is without Jesus Christ we cannot know God (John 14:6). And without knowing God, the Creator, there is no way to know what God has curiously wrought us for. God has a specific plan for each and every one of His people.

Jer. 1:5 "Before I formed thee in the belly, I knew thee;
and before thou camest forth out of the womb I sanc-
tified thee, [and] I ordained thee a prophet unto the
nations."

Here we have God speaking to Jeremiah. What I find interesting is this
verse is the very first statement God makes to Jeremiah. (God knows
exactly how people think.). He knew the first thing Jeremiah would do
is question what God knows about him. See we, as living souls, think
we have the proper approach to life and money figured out. God tries
to set us straight in Isa. 55:8. He assertively states, "...my thoughts are
not your thoughts, neither are your ways my ways." God knew exactly
what He created Jeremiah to do. He knew when to send him and He
knew who to send him to. He "formed you in the belly" too, believer!

John 15:16 "Ye have not chosen me, but I have chosen
you, and ordained you, that ye should go and bring
forth fruit, and [that] your fruit should remain: that
whatsoever ye shall ask of the Father in my name, he
may give it you."

In this verse, Jesus is talking to his disciples. When we observe Jesus
teaching the disciples, He is really teaching what we call "the
Church." Many of us think we "found God." We use expressions like,
"Since I've found God, my life is not the same." Did anybody read
the verse above? Jesus is basically saying, "You did not choose me. I
chose you, and not only that, but I chose you for a specific purpose
— to be fruitful. Does that sound familiar?

Eph. 2:10 "For we are his workmanship, created in
Christ Jesus unto good works, which God hath before
ordained that we should walk in them."

Here Paul is writing to the saints at Ephesus. He is trying to get the Ephesians to understand that God does not make mistakes. Here we go...

Work-man-ship

Work means mental or physical effort directed toward a goal or purpose. *Man* refers to male and female living souls. The suffix -*ship* means the quality, state, or condition. Bringing it home, mankind was originally expressly created to be in the constant condition or state of working to fulfill God's purpose in the earth. That is the crux of the whole gospel. The gospel is all about a family reunion.

Created in Christ Jesus

Being born again through the acceptance of Jesus Christ as Lord and Savior makes us new creatures (2 Cor. 5:17) and restores us to workmanship status. The Word of God is now our foundation and the expectation is we will do good works.

Before Ordained

Notice this was God's intent when he drew up the plans to create mankind. It didn't just happen. It's not a coincidence.

So we find that God intricately designed us for a specific purpose. The way we find that purpose is through cultivating a relationship with Him through the Holy Spirit. He has made each and every one of us for this moment and this time. Let's see what global economics can teach us about the value of being special.

Global Economics

In global economics there is an idea called the *law of comparative advantage* that works around the notion of specialization. In its barest form, it states that all nations would be better off if individual nations specialized in producing goods for which they are the low-opportunity-cost producer. In turn, they should trade for the goods for which they are the high-opportunity-cost producer. All nations are richer and happier when they specialize in what they are the best at and trade for what they are less good at.

This is a profound idea. Everyone is not the best at everything. Now many folks may be good at a lot of things, but only a few people are the best. The math of the law of comparative advantage emphatically proves specialization is better for everyone. Singing is a natural example. Some people were created to be soloists, while others were created to sing background. Others belong in the congregation singing as low as possible. How many people know we are all better off when the soloists sing lead, the background singers sing in the choir, and the congregation sings from their seats? Has anyone ever been in a situation where the singing is out of order? It is not pretty. Everyone is certainly not better off. A natural soloist extends almost no effort to be excellent at what he or she does; the natural soloist is a low-opportunity-cost producer. Whereas there is an evident struggle when a non-soloist (a high-opportunity-cost producer) attempts a solo.

What we can glean from this trip down economics lane is that everyone has unique, God-given talents and abilities that lead to success and wealth. Prov. 18:16 announces, "A man's gift maketh room for him, and bringeth him before great men." By no means am I suggesting you can only be good at one thing. I am also not saying you cannot develop and improve your assorted gifts, talents, and abilities. However, I am pointing out that God created each of us fearfully and wonderfully. He created you to specialize in some areas of life. I specialize in leadership, writing, preaching, personal finance, singing, and worship. I plan to add to the repertoire as the Spirit leads. When we individually get into a place of communion with the Father through the Holy Spirit, everyone is richer and happier because God reveals our specialties. Our gifts, talents, and abilities bring us into awesome opportunities and lead to wealth and fulfillment.

Starting Where I Am

Many passages in the Bible, besides the ones above, allude to the fact that God has the end in mind before He ever creates the beginning. The reality is that most effective planners operate in the same manner. For example, I research defense stocks as part of my everyday job. One of the companies I cover, The Boeing Company, has come up with a concept plane named the Sonic Cruiser. Boeing's engineers have spent (and will continue to spend) months and months designing every intricate detail of that plane. The end result will be the finished plane. The design is finished when the drawings are complete, but the plane must still be physically built in the factory. God works the same way. He never does anything without a plan (we will dissect that later). Then He works the plan. He expects the same approach from us.

Now that we can see God's plan for us is unique, it is not hard to also see that God can meet us right where we are in our lives. No matter what we have done up until now, God is still faithful to forgive and restore us, if we are willing to order our lives according to His Word. As it relates to our financial resources, this is where we can begin our journey into destroying the digger mentality and walking in the planter lifestyle God intended for us from the foundation of the worlds. Some of us are staring at a mountain of debt. Some of us are tired of living check-to-check. Some of us are afraid to invest because we do not understand how money works. Some of us have dreams and goals but lack the patience and dedication necessary to see them through. Regardless of your current predicament, God's Word holds the key to your deliverance. The Word of God ministers to us on a personal level. God knows exactly what you specialize in. He knows where you have been and where you are going. You just have to make a quality decision to start where you are. Now!

SEEDS FOR YOUR SOIL

The Value of Man: Psalm 8 and John 3:1-21

1. List the earthly things that God turned over to the care of mankind. Is anything missing?

2. What did God give back to man through Jesus that the Adams forfeited in Gen. 3:19-22?

The Originality of Man: Psalm 138 and Psalm 139

1. What is it that God does not know about you? What are you worried about again?

God Chose Me: John 15

1. What should branches do? What is the result when a branch does not fulfill that purpose? What is the result when a branch does fulfill that purpose?

2. What did God choose you for?

CHAPTER 2

I Don't Know Money

How what I Don't Know Can Destroy Me

Lack of Knowledge

Just the other day I was talking on the phone with a good friend. We discussed what was happening in each of our lives, and, as usual, we started talking about money. (Hey...we're MBAS!) Anyway, we had both recently attempted to help people with their personal finances and had experienced similar frustrations. During that conversation, my friend made a poignant observation: Most people just don't know how money works. That remark weighed heavily in my spirit as I was right in the middle of writing this book. I thought to myself, "How can we help people to understand how money works?"

Before we begin, understand the word *know* means to be aware of the truth or factuality of; to have a practical understanding of. So when we say most people do not *know* money, we are saying people are not aware of the truth about money and people definitely do not have a practical or effective understanding of how to use money. I can hear the comments now: "I know how to use money. I was just in Sak's the other day." That is exactly what I am talking about. We know how to use money in one way — spend it. Careless spending is the same as digging. So what does God think about the concept of knowledge?

> *Hos. 4:6* "My people are destroyed for lack of knowledge: because thou has rejected knowledge, I will also reject thee, thou shalt be no priest to me: seeing thou hast forgotten the law of thy God, I will also forget thy children."

What we find here is God's people are ineffective because they lack knowledge. But knowledge is available. The scripture says, "because thou has rejected knowledge." When we do not make use of the knowledge available to us, we are rejecting or refusing that knowledge. We can safely conclude it is impossible to properly use money without the knowledge of how money works. Impossible means it is not going to happen. Just because we have attended college does not mean we know how to use money. Just because we were raised with a great amount of street knowledge does not mean we know how to use money. Just because we have purchased quite a few items does not mean we know how to use money. There are people, books, videos, and classes available that possess everything we need to know about taking control of our finances. Peeling back the pages of this book is a fantastic step in the right direction.

The Effect of Knowledge

The first thing knowledge does when it shows up at your doorstep is it begins to change your thinking, which in turn changes your approach. Knowing opens the door for the successful use of money.

> *Prov. 24:3-4* "Through wisdom is an house builded;

and by understanding it is established: And by knowledge shall the chambers be filled with all precious and pleasant riches."

For practical purposes we will use some simple definitions my pastor often uses to distinguish between wisdom, understanding, and knowledge. Wisdom is the "how." Understanding is the "when and where." Knowledge is the "what." In this verse, we find wisdom (the Word of God) provides the foundation; understanding (accepting what is in the Word of God) provides stability; and knowledge (knowing what to do) leads to prosperity. The problem is most of us do not know what to do with money so we do what we see other people do — spend it. I have news for you. Prosperity is not found in spending. This chapter provides the knowledge about money that will help you begin to take control of your financial situation.

> *Prov. 11:9* "A hypocrite with [his] mouth destroyeth his neighbor: but through knowledge shall the just be delivered."

This proverb underscores the point that knowledge precedes deliverance. People do not live check to check because they like it. People live check to check because they do not know how to do anything else. People generally *do* what they *know*. How could they not? What would I look like if I tried to build a house without first learning what it takes to build a house? People are stuck in the American-dream cycle because they do not know anything else to do. Therefore, we get a car note, get a house note, get a dog, and have two-and-a-half kids. We then work at a job to pay for our entire infrastructure. Something is missing, but we do not quite know what it is. Does anyone know how to get me out of this?

Top Two Areas of Ignorance

As a person who grew up in a church environment, I can say two issues were seldom talked about and thus not taught well — sex and money. Now these are the two biggest issues separating man from God, yet the church community has largely ignored them. Again, the lack of knowledge results in ineffective behavior. Why have these subjects traditionally not been taught? Here is my two cents. Number one: many "church" people are acting totally against the will of God in these areas, making for a very uncomfortable discussion (especially if you want to keep the church full). Number two: once the truth about these issues comes into a person's life it will have one of two effects. The truth will either change one's life and draw that person closer to God or it will frustrate a person and move him or her further from God. Either way makes for an uncomfortable experience. We will not touch the sex thing with this book, but I believe the improper use of sex is probably the number one reason why people cannot build a relationship with God. We will spend our time on what I tout as the number two reason why people cannot find God in their lives — money.

What Is Money?

We deal with the money issue like it is a surprise to God that there is money in the earth. Money is a resource, pure and simple. It is the universal exchange system in the earth. You are currently reading money, sitting on money, wearing money, thinking about money, working for money, and so forth. Money is the one of the only things we all have in common. We can do next to nothing of physical significance in the earth realm without some paper, cheddar, bread, moolah, cash, or Benjimans. Money gives us the right to claim pieces of the earth!

> *Eccl. 10:19* "A feast is made for laughter, and wine maketh merry: but money answereth all things."

18

This illustrates the universal nature of money. In other words, if you have money you can have a feast or you can buy some wine or you can do both. Money is always accepted.

The Purpose of Money

> *Gen. 1:29* "And God said, Behold, I have given you (mankind) every herb bearing seed, which [is] upon the face of all the earth, and every tree, in the which [is] the fruit of a tree yielding seed; to you it shall be for meat."

Is this verse talking about money too? You bet it is. Prior to this verse, God blessed or empowered mankind to be the steward of the earth and then gave us instructions on how to operate in the earth. In this verse, God is identifying the resources we have at our disposal to carry out the instructions given in Gen. 1:28. (Note the seed was upon the face of all the earth. That sounds like abundance or what we referred to earlier as the concept of increase. God designed all seeds to exponentially produce after their own kind.) The phrase "to you it shall be for meat" is interesting. That word *meat* means food or sustenance (that which sustains), provision, means, resources, and wealth. Now answer this question: Where does money come from? How many people know money does actually grow on trees?

Did we miss that? God empowered us, instructed us, and equipped us with everything needed to live in abundance. God expects us to set up shop down here and operate it like He operates heaven. If you do not own anything of value in the earth, how are you going to dominate it? How do you make things happen on a grand scale in the natural? How many people think the answer is money? How many people think it's having faith? Money is how we accomplish pretty much every natural task set before us. Faith is what allows God to move beyond the natural on our behalf. If you really think about my position, you will be hard pressed to come up with an example that does not involve the use of money. The purpose of money is not to pay your bills. The purpose of money is to administer the things of God right now while we are on earth. And when we are walking in God's specific purpose for us, God allows us to access all the things we could ever need and much more.

Money Is Evil?

This money issue has been taught incorrectly for so long that I used to think God thought money was evil. I would think to myself, "How come we need money for everything when God thinks it is evil?" That is exactly why it pays to study the Word of God on your own.

> *1 Tim. 6:7, 10* "For we brought nothing into [this] world, [and it is] certain we can carry nothing out...For the love of money is the root of all evil: which while some coveted after, they have erred from the faith, and pierced themselves through with many sorrows."

Man, I don't believe I thought money was evil. This passage is clearly speaking about having a proper relationship with money. Money is just a thing. Look at that passage closely.

No Thing

This passage makes two distinct points about "no thing." We brought "no thing" in and we take "no thing" out. That implies "thing" is to be used properly while we are in the earth because there is "no thing" outside of the earth realm.

Love

When we think of the word love, we often think of a touchy-feely emotional high. Well, let's kill that myth. According to the Bible

(1 Corinthians 13), that feeling has nothing to do with love. Love is not a feeling. Love is a constant state of preferential treatment despite how we feel. Love is giving. Love is a choice.

So how can we love money? Take a mental trip with me. How many people spend the majority of the week working at a job they are not happy with? How many times a week do you wake up and say to yourself: "I don't feel like going to work?" So why are you still working there? That's right...you want to get paid! We prefer working at that job and continuing to receive a check to seeking God's will for our lives and building our sources of income from that revelation.

All Evil

This is a bold statement. I mean this verse plainly says the love of money leads to all evil — every single thing God calls evil. Understand *evil* just means against God. Remember money is just a word for the phrase "universal natural resource."

Back to the Adams...What caused the Adams to disconnect the entire human race from God? What was the root of all evil? They loved the earth more than the counsel of God. This was a violation of trust. They trusted in that which was made rather than trusting in the Maker of all resources. When we learn to truly love God, we will trust Him to guide and direct our respective career paths. He will ensure we receive enough natural resources in whatever state we find ourselves in (that is, money) to accomplish all those things within His will we have been dreaming of.

Effect of Covetousness

When we love or give preferential treatment to natural resources it results in two states of being. First, it causes us to "err from the faith." There is no way to walk by faith when our focus and energy is on how we can get that next dollar. Remember, faith moves beyond natural resources. Second, it results in "many sorrows." How many people are always worried about how they are going to pay their bills; how they are going to get out of debt; or how they are going to pay for their kids? This is sorrow!

A Proper Relationship with Money

> *Luke 16:13* "No servant can serve two masters: for either he will hate the one, and love the other; or else he will hold to the one, and despise the other. Ye cannot serve God and mammon."

God does not condemn money. He is concerned about our relationship with money. When we are worried about paying our bills or buying some more stuff, then we are not sensitive to God's purpose concerning us. In fact, if we don't learn to trust God, we will never reach our potential partially due to the fact we do not have the natural resources (in our present state) necessary to do what God wants us to do with our lives. That amount is not currently in our bank account. Consequently, God desires for us to keep our minds on His capabilities and resources, not our own. Remember, He made all resources.

When we talk about trust, we are speaking of a total commitment to and dependence on God. Many of us are committed to our jobs simply because they pay us. We serve our employers because of money. We depend on that paycheck. We get comfortable in our jobs and generate bills that will not allow us to quit even when we realize we are severely out of place and unhappy. It is so subtle, but we essentially exist to make and spend money, not to serve God's purpose for mankind. This is far from a suggestion to quit your job so God can give you some money for "trusting" Him. God wants you to work to get money. He just wants your work to line up with His will and purpose for your life. That is where you will find the most satisfaction and that is how God obtains glory.

In Luke 14:16-24, Jesus teaches a parable about a man (God) who made a great supper (the Word of God) and invited many people (diggers) to come and partake. The message the man sent to his invitees was this: Come, because all things are ready now (everything you need to live abundantly is prepared right now). Now, one would think these folks would drop what they were doing to participate in this feast of abundance. However, check out the excuses from some of the guests: I just bought some land and I must go see it; I just bought some cattle and I must go tend to them; and I just got married so I don't think I will be able to make it. What do these excuses have in common? Come on. Say it with me: money! This is a relationship problem. These guests did not recognize the nature of the invitation — all things are ready now! In other words, I have given you access to everything you need so why are you worried about the money? Let us finish the lesson. The master of the house became angry with his original invitees and commanded his servant to take the invite to the streets. Find anyone you can who is willing to partake in My feast of abundance. My initial invitees are cut off. They apparently think their money is enough.

Money is just a resource and God put more than enough resources in the earth for all of mankind to live abundantly. When the focus of all of our time and effort is on making money in an occupation that makes us miserable simply to pay bills and buy more stuff, then we have undoubtedly put money in God's place. God knows we need money. He is the one who gave us the talents and abilities to make money. Many of us, however, do not have the right attitude toward money or the way to go about generating it, which in turn leads to mismanagement of resources and dependence on the natural things that God created.

How Money Works in the Real World

Before there was money, there was something we call barter. Barter happens when I exchange something I have that you want for something you have that I want. As you can imagine, this scenario grew old as people had to expend so much time and effort to find people with items they wanted. At the same time, they had to make sure they had something the other person would be willing to trade for. Enter money. Money became the medium of exchange that allowed anyone to trade anything with anyone else. It became a universal exchange standard.

Money, in our society, flows like this[E].

1. The Federal Reserve writes a check for say $100 million to purchase securities from a brokerage house. The brokerage house, in turn, deposits the check at Piggy Bank, increasing Piggy's cash position.
2. Piggy must set aside a certain amount (let's say 10 percent) to meet Federal Reserve requirements and can lend the remaining $90 million to its customers. The Adams borrow $200,000 from Piggy to buy a new house. The Abrahams, our sellers, deposit the money in their bank, Blessed.
3. Now Blessed Bank has $180,000 (remember the reserve requirement) to lend to its customers. Mary comes to Blessed to borrow $30,000 for transportation. The mule salesman deposits Mary's check in Bethlehem National.
4. Bethlehem National now has $27,000 it can loan to its customers.

This short four-step process has created $190,207,000! If you keep going...well, you do the math! Consumers who buy stuff they cannot afford multiply money through the system! I just told you something.

Time Value of Money
I am only going to scratch the surface of this concept. Minister Shun-

drawn will handle this is great detail in *Start Planting!* Money has a time value as long as it can be invested at some positive rate of return. Through this principle, we get concepts like compound interest, future value, and present value. *Compounding* is the process of accumulating interest over a period of time. *Future value* is the amount an investment would grow to after one or more periods. *Present value* is the current value of some future cash flow discounted at a given interest rate. (Can you tell I majored in accounting and finance?) Understanding these concepts will help us transform our digger mentality to one of productivity.

Armed with the concept of compounding, we want to deal with a notion called *the rule of 72*. This idea gives us a rule of thumb that will allow us to estimate how long it takes for money to double. The rule says, "If you want to know how many years it will take you to double your money, take the number 72 and divide it by the interest rate you expect to return." Rearranging the concept, we can find out what rate of return we need to double our money over a given period of time. For example, if we want to double an investment of $100,000 in five years, we would have to earn 72 divided by five or 14.4 percent annually. Conversely, if we hold $500 in a savings account earning one percent, it will take us 72 years to turn that $500 into $1,000. Remember this concept, we are coming back to it.

Seeds for Your Soil

Danger of Lack of Knowledge: Hosea 4 and Prov. 1:1-7

1. What is the result of lack of knowledge? How does this relate to our finances?

2. What is the beginning of knowledge? Why is that relevant to the believer?

Money Is Not Evil: 1 Timothy 6

1. How much stuff did we bring into this world with us?

2. What types of things should the believer be following after and why?

3. Whom should we trust and what did He give us richly to enjoy?

Relating to Money: Luke 14:7-24

1. According to Luke 14:7-11, what should be our position as we approach the issues of life?

2. According to Luke 14:12-14, what should be our approach to giving of our substance?

3. According to Luke 14:15-24, what should be our focus as it relates to the Source of money and money itself?

CHAPTER 3

OWE NO MAN ANYTHING

Why Debt Is Not in the Will of God

Man and His Mortgage Mentality

Debt results directly from the digger or mortgage mentality. Talk about a nasty four-letter word. The word *debt* means sin, trespass, or something owed. Earlier, we learned the digger mentality led mankind to sin against God. Man had now literally become debt. All people after the Adams' fall are born with a sin, or debt, nature automatically. Did anybody get that? Man is now born with a natural inclination toward debt. Instead of possessing the nature of God given to man originally in Gen. 2:7, man chose the opposite nature — one of debt. Mankind is now indebted to the works of the Devil and to the works of his own flesh. The Bible declares we belong to what we give ourselves to (Rom. 6:16). Mankind mortgaged their ability to live a truly successful life in the earth realm. In essence, mankind gave up their lives to service their debt.

God thought so much of mankind that He spent four thousand years preparing man to be in a position to receive the release from his debt. Has anyone ever heard the phrase "the wages of sin is death"? How many people know you have to have a life in order to die? See, God initially gave us eternal life and we chose death through disobedience. But Jesus died that we might live again. Well, what does that mean? God's intent before the foundation of the world was for man to live an abundant and prosperous life forever right here in the earth based on the Word or instructions of God. For God to be able to position man to fulfill that purpose, He had to pay the wages of sin, which is death. Since God is a holy God, just any old death would not be adequate to fully restore man to God's original standard of holiness. In the Old Testament, we find man offering all types of sacrifices to God to cover sin in an effort to cultivate a relationship with a holy God. But God had prepared the ultimate sacrifice — Jesus Christ. That is why God says things like "you were bought with a price" (1 Cor. 6:20 and 7:23). The holy sacrifice or death of Jesus erased the debt of man. Jesus paved the way for God to again equip mankind with His very nature, putting mankind in a position to fulfill his original purpose. The Holy Spirit communicates with our new spirit to move us to God's projected destination for us.

God's View on Debt

I can sum up this section quickly: God hates debt! Debt is opposite to the nature of God. Let us take a look at some of the words associated with debt in the Bible — bondage, yoke, and burden. *Bondage* is the Greek word *douleia* (doo-li'-ah), which means the condition of being a slave. A *yoke* is simply a mechanism that ties two things to each other. It is commonly used to refer to a heavy bar used to tie two oxen together for work. The Bible also used the word *yoke* to describe the marriage relationship as well as the relationship between a master and servant. The key to grasping the power of the word lies in the understanding that a yoke is extremely difficult to remove. *Burden* is the Greek word *baros* (bar'-os) and it denotes a weight or anything that makes a demand on one's resources. Debt makes a serious demand on your resources — time, effort, and money.

So what is God's official view on debt? God desires to deliver us from debt because it is so far from His purpose for mankind.

> *Isa. 14:24-27* "The Lord of hosts hath sworn, saying, Surely as I have thought, so shall it come to pass; and as I have purposed, [so] shall it stand. That I will break the Assyrian in my land, and upon my mountains tread him under foot: then shall his yoke depart from off them, and his burden depart from off their shoulders. This [is] the purpose that is purposed on the whole earth: and this [is] the hand that is stretched out upon all nations. For the Lord of hosts hath purposed, and who shall disannul [it]? and his hand [is] stretched out, and who shall turn it back?"

The Assyrians

These people were a militant bunch. War was their primary activity. How many people know the opposite of peace is war? How many people know you can substitute the words strife, envy, or confusion for the word war? In addition to being warriors, the Assyrians were astute businessmen and completely intolerant of other religious beliefs. They thought they knew it all.

Sovereign God

Do we realize what the word *sovereign* means? To be sovereign one must have supreme authority. In other words, no one can veto that person's word no matter how they feel. God declares that what He wants will happen and what He purposes shall stand! It's like God saying, "It doesn't matter what you think! I am the sovereign God!"

Debt Destruction

God purposed to destroy the root of the people's debt, which was confusion, a false sense of what success is, and a lack of dependence on or relationship with the true and living God. He declared that He would break the Assyrian that personified those very traits.

The Whole Earth and All Nations

Don't miss this! We know God is speaking specifically to the children of Israel through Isaiah in this passage, however, please do not miss how the Holy Spirit is working this. After God declared the root of the debt would be destroyed for the children of Israel, He stated, "This is the purpose that is purposed on the whole earth." Did we catch that? In other words, His intent is to demolish the root of all debt for all people. All I can say is wow.

God is concerned about each and every soul He created. No one group of people has a lock on God. God has established His Word and it will stand forever. All things that are not aligned with His Word will be burned. This includes the digger or mortgage mentality. But God was not just worried about the mortgage mentality itself. He destroyed the root of the mortgage mentality — confusion, false sense of success, and a lack of relationship with Jesus Christ or His Word. The Truth demolishes confusion, defines success, and corrects behavior!

Debt as a Hindrance to Destiny: Mortgage Mentality after Deliverance

Rom. 8:15 "For ye have not received the spirit of bondage again to fear; but ye have received the Spirit of adoption, whereby we cry, Abba, Father."

God is trying to clear something up for us here. Once we have accepted the Lord Jesus Christ and received the Holy Spirit, we must recognize we have been birthed with a new spirit that is about abundance, not bondage. Once we grasp that concept, we overcome the mortgage mentality through the Word of God. We are transformed (changed into something different than what was there before) by the renewing of the mind (Rom. 12:2). The problem is debt is so ingrained in the psyche of people they cannot think properly. We will pick up on the concept of thinking properly in the next chapter. For now let us spend some time looking at the effect of having a mortgage mentality after being delivered from debt.

Case Study: The Children of Israel

The children of Israel spent almost four hundred years in bondage to Egypt. They complained and whined. They received a great promise from God. They were miraculously delivered from their slavery in Egypt. They came out of Egypt with great wealth. They were sustained in the wilderness by God. Then they complained and whined because things weren't the way they wanted. They refused to rely on the Word of God. They missed the destination and died in the wilderness.

Here we have a people whose destiny was the Promised Land, but due to a mortgage mentality they died in the wilderness without ever reaching that destiny. At one point in the story, the people even talked of finding another leader and going back to Egypt (Numb. 14:4). What kind of mentality would make a person want to go back to slavery after being made free? Debt has that same effect in a believer's life. We can miss our destiny when we harbor a mortgage mentality.

Slaving Away

Prov. 22:7 "The rich ruleth over the poor, and the borrower [is] servant to the lender."

In the magnificent world of finance, we have a phrase for companies that make periodic payments on their outstanding debts. We call it "servicing the debt." Let's work with that word *servant*. In our context, it is the Hebrew word *ebed* (eh'-bed), meaning one in bondage. We know bondage refers to the condition of being a slave. This proverb tells us plainly that when we borrow we become a slave to our lender. That is not hard to see. Is it?

Not clear? How many people have a mortgage? How many people have a car note? How many people have student loans? How many people have credit card debt? Okay, now that I have everyone's attention, let me illustrate the point. What is one of the primary reasons many of us continue to work at our respective jobs? Say it with me: To pay off some of this debt. We literally work forty to sixty hours a week to service our debts. We slave away to finance the lifestyle of our lenders. We do the work and our lenders get paid. It's just like slavery!

This ought not be! We, as believers, are free to walk in the power and authority God gave man in the Garden of Eden. The children of Israel and modern day black Americans show us that just because you free a slave from his or her condition does not mean that slave knows how to exercise his or her freedom. Knowledge is what separates the haves and the have-nots. Knowledge is what transforms a mortgage mentality into one of productivity.

Uncontrolled Spending: Debt in Sheep's Clothing

Prov. 21:20 "[There is] treasure to be desired and oil in the dwelling of the wise; but a foolish man spendeth it up."

How many people know debt is merely the result of a lack of discipline in spending decisions? At the time this proverb was penned, treasure and oil represented the pinnacle of natural wealth. (Some would argue the same stands today.) This proverb suggests that treasure is desirable. That tells us natural possessions are not evil. The proverb also tells us that there are resources in the household of a person who exercises wisdom. However, it cautions us that a foolish person will spend every dime. We know from our personal experiences with credit cards that a foolish person will even spend what he or she does not have. A foolish person says things like, "I only live once so I might as well enjoy myself now." What a shortsighted stance! What about the people around you? What about the people that come after you? What are you going to do if your job goes away? Are you adequately prepared? What about the future?

> *Prov. 29:3* "Whoso loveth wisdom rejoiceth his father: but he that keepeth company with harlots spendeth [his] substance."

Are we offended by the phrase "keepeth company with harlots"? We do not think this verse is referring to us. Do we? Let's get an understanding.

Keeps Company
This is merely talking about being in continual fellowship. I know many of us have heard this phrase: if you hang around nine broke people, you are bound to be the tenth one. This should make a whole lot of sense to us. If I harbor a mortgage mentality, then all I can teach you is how to be in debt. I cannot teach what I do not practice.

Harlots
This word makes many of us immediately think of adultery, but I want to challenge us on that quick assumption. *Harlot* is the Hebrew word *zanah* (zaw-naw'), which can also be translated wanton. This

explains why *zanah* also refers to being a harlot and even sometimes being a whore. Wanton means undisciplined; unruly. It is lack of discipline that causes a person to "spend his or her substance." If you keep company with undisciplined and unfaithful people, your substance will quickly disappear.

Overspending is digging. Do you have a handle on your spending? How much money do you spend on food per month? Entertainment? Gasoline? Miscellaneous? The Debt-Cancellation/Spending-Reduction Plan in the back of the book will help you answer these questions accurately.

You Cannot Afford It

Some of you may need to face a reality: you cannot afford yourself at this present moment. If you are struggling every month to pay your bills, you cannot afford what you are doing. You need to cut back. If you are worrying about where money is going to come from to pay for stuff you are already using, you have a bunch of stuff you cannot afford. You need to take it back.

> *Prov. 22:26-27* "Be not thou [one] of them that strike hands, [or] of them that are sureties for debts. If thou hast nothing to pay, why should he take away thy bed from under thee?"

I love this one. "Strike hands" is actually just referring to shaking hands with someone as people often do to strike a deal. You know we shake the loan officer's hand for a mortgage. We shake the car dealer's hand for a beamer. It means thanks for the money and the stuff — I'll gladly pay you back with interest! Notice this though: we do not really own anything. We owe everything. How many people know the car dealer will come get that borrowed car when you lose the ability to keep paying for it? This verse says, "Obviously, you cannot afford this item. After all, you're borrowing the money for it. Why would you put yourself in a bad position like that?"

Reasons People Overspend

Personal Finance for Dummies (a must have for all those who truly want to gain control of their financial situations) lists several reasons why people overspend. I have altered their list slightly for purposes of our discussion.

1. Credit Cards (Minimum Payment Mentality) — We will explore the warped math of having this mentality in just a few short sections.

2. Cars (Monthly Payment Mentality) — This is subtle debt violation because many of us think of cars as an asset. I cannot necessarily argue with that conclusion. I would just say it is a depreciating asset. Borrowing for a depreciating asset also results in warped math. This is a touchy issue since most of us "have" to have a car and "might as well" get something we like.

3. Peer Pressure (Keeping Up with the Joneses) — This is largely a self-esteem problem. When we feel the urge to amass possessions equal to or better than the people's around us, we need to check for one of the devil's main tools: fear. We cannot walk around afraid of what others may think or say. We cannot live life worrying about what others are doing. Fear is the antifaith. Where there is fear there is no faith. We must exhibit confidence in what God says concerning us, for God has not given us a spirit of fear (2 Tim. 1:7).

4. Feeling Good (False Peace) — A lot of us spend to make ourselves feel good. Now I am not knocking that in and of itself. I like returning from the store with something new, and it does make me feel good. What we want to deal with is the notion of substituting the emotions of feeling good with the wholeness that comes in the salvation package. We are talking about people who spend money they do not have because buying things basically gives them a false sense of peace. A month later, the bill shows up. We know how that story turns out. Right?

5. Addiction (Missing Peace) — This is a deeper version of the feeling-good problem. Many of us spend to feel good and literally cannot stop ourselves. Shopping is some folks' alcohol or drug. However, many of us refuse to identify it as an addiction. We need deliverance. We have yet to experience God's peace so we look for it in the mall. God's peace begins with the saving of one's soul and manifests as one obeys God's Word, especially concerning money.

6. No Financial Goals (Lack of Purpose) — Without counsel purposes fail (Prov. 15:22). Without vision people perish (Prov. 29:18). These are hallmark pearls of wisdom. Lack of purpose leads to misdirected use. Many of us recklessly waste money because we have no plan or purpose for its use. We do not even understand the purpose of money in our lives. We believe it is just for accumulating stuff so that is all we do.

When to Use Debt

Now I know that sounds ludicrous considering I spent most of this chapter talking about avoiding debt all together. But my aim is to provide practical financial solutions that line up with the Word of God. One thing about debt in this day and age is it can be a form of investment. And practically speaking, most of us do not have the cash available to finance the expenditures I am going to mention. There are three primary ways (there may be others) debt can be used an investment — real estate, education and entrepreneurship.

Real Estate

Many people borrow to obtain their first home. Now the reality is the bank actually owns your home, but at least you retain the rights to sell it for a profit as long as you keep your payments current. Unfortunately, most first-time buyers bite off more than they can chew when they purchase their first home. This syndrome is known in the investment industry as being house poor. Typically your broker tells you the maximum loan you can qualify for in an effort to sell you a home at the highest price you all can agree on. The result is you end up locking up a significant portion of your monthly income. This situation is exacerbated if you underestimated the maintenance costs of the property, which occurs frequently. Many end up drowning under the weight of their monthly debt obligations and emergency expenses even though the home is supposed to be an investment. For a great majority of us, the previously described scenario prevents home ownership from being the great investment that most financial experts believe it to be. In fact, home ownership can act more like a liability than a great investment when coupled with an inadequate financial foundation.

Alternatively, there is the option of purchasing rental property as a first home. Owner-occupied property is a path of wealth creation rarely traveled by the have-nots. My wife and I are pursuing this option. Many people shun the idea of being a landlord, but we recognize that to become independently wealthy, we must put in work early in life. We plan to buy something cheaper than what we qualify for and live rent free or close to it. Now that's a great investment! You eliminate a huge monthly obligation while someone else builds the equity in your property. You are still responsible for managing the property and processes, but everything in life costs you something. Right?

Education

Unfortunately for many of us, our trust fund (yes...I am being sarcastic) did not adequately cover the expenses for our higher education. U.S. Census Bureau statistics reveal that a person's willingness to increase his or her education directly affects his or her earning power in life. Now, of course, there are exceptions to the rule, but more education usually equals more money. Borrowing to finance a quality education can be a great investment in your future earnings potential. For example, I now make over two-and-a-half times more on a net basis than what I made just two years prior to attending graduate school.

Entrepreneurship

Another path less traveled is that of business ownership. Many entrepreneurs must borrow money to make their ideas come to life. The creditworthiness of the business owner, the assets of the company, and the viability of the business concept affect the ability to borrow. Borrowing money is also cheaper than giving up an ownership stake in your company, especially when your idea takes off. Most independently wealthy people did not make their fortune working for someone else.

When Not to Use Debt

Notice that credit cards did not make our list of when to use debt. Am I suggesting you do not use credit cards? No. Here are three quick rules for using credit cards:

1. Use them only for convenience and points, miles, or other perks.
2. Pay off your balance every month.
3. Only charge amounts for which you already have the cash on hand to pay.

Another popular use of debt that did not make our list is cosigning.

> *Prov. 11:15* "He that is surety for a stranger shall smart [for it]: and he that hateth suretyship is sure."

> *Prov. 17:18* "A man void of understanding striketh hands, [and] becometh surety in the presence of his friend."

These proverbs completely support God's outlook on debt. They are specifically referring to cosigning either for a stranger or a friend. "Smart" refers to crying out with a loud voice. How many people know living under the weight of somebody else's debt makes you want to scream? Cosigning a lifestyle another person obviously cannot afford results in mental discomfort. God does not believe in welfare. He believes in work. The person who is opposed to debt is sure. He is not worried. This person is not just saying, "I hate being in debt." He or she does not assume debt. Whatever he or she has is totally paid for. Now that's comfort!

Revisiting the Rule of 72: Bad Math!

In the last chapter we talked about this infamous rule. Let us now see how it applies to the credit card game. Suppose we bought a $300 leather jacket at Wilson's. The great thing about the jacket is that it was on sale — 20 percent off — so it will only cost us $240! We put the jacket on our Visa, which has an annual percentage rate (APR) of 18 percent. Now, we really could not afford the jacket, but it was a must have! We assume we can afford to pay $15 per month until we get some extra money to pay it off. So how does the math work?

Month	Balance	Interest @ 1.5% (APR/12)	Monthly Payment
1	$ 240.00	$ 3.60	$ (15.00)
2	$ 228.60	$ 3.43	$ (15.00)
3	$ 217.03	$ 3.26	$ (15.00)
4	$ 205.28	$ 3.08	$ (15.00)
5	$ 193.36	$ 2.90	$ (15.00)
6	$ 181.26	$ 2.72	$ (15.00)
7	$ 168.98	$ 2.53	$ (15.00)
8	$ 156.52	$ 2.35	$ (15.00)
9	$ 143.87	$ 2.16	$ (15.00)
10	$ 131.02	$ 1.97	$ (15.00)
11	$ 117.99	$ 1.77	$ (15.00)
12	$ 104.76	$ 1.57	$ (15.00)
13	$ 91.33	$ 1.37	$ (15.00)
14	$ 77.70	$ 1.17	$ (15.00)
15	$ 63.87	$ 0.96	$ (15.00)
16	$ 49.82	$ 0.75	$ (15.00)
17	$ 35.57	$ 0.53	$ (15.00)
18	$ 21.10	$ 0.32	$ (21.42)
Total			$ (276.42)

What just happened? We just paid $276.42 (approximately 15 percent more) for a $240 jacket that was on sale. It took us one-and-a-half years to pay it off. Furthermore, we only wore the jacket eight out of the eighteen months we were paying for it! That 15 percent number should startle us. There is a concept in finance called opportunity cost. The name of the concept pretty much explains its definition. Basically, when we decide to use money for a specific purpose we forego the opportunity to use the money for other purposes. For example, the average annual return on the stock market since the late '20s is around 10 percent, which means if we would have invested our $240 over an "average" one-and-a-half year period, we would have $278 in our pocket. That is a 16 percent absolute return. When we couple our fictional $38 gain with our real ($36) loss we observe a $74 swing. This essentially means that we paid $314 for a $300 jacket that was on sale. See the bad math?

What does this have to do with the rule of 72? How many people know that people who shop generally don't just buy one thing over an eighteen-month period? Imagine there were a few more things on sale over that eighteen-month period. Imagine our credit card bill is now $5,000. Remember we can only afford to pay $15 a month unless we miraculously get some extra money to pay it off. Using the rule of 72, let us examine how long it will take for our new $5,000 credit card bill to double to $10,000. To simplify this example, we will assume we cannot afford to make *any* monthly payments. Here we go...72 divided by 18 percent APR equals 48 months. In just four short years, we will owe $10,000 for stuff that cost $5,000. Mind you in four years we have also bought a whole lot of other stuff! Can we see the vicious cycle?

This type of behavior plays out over and over again in many people's lives. It stems from lack of knowledge and lack of discretion. Many of us do not understand how money flows so we satisfy each and every whim that comes to us. We do not understand the purpose of money so we build our lives on consumption. We do not understand how we should relate to money so we do almost anything to get it and almost everything to keep from giving it away.

Getting to the Root of Debt

When we are facing problems we often address the symptoms of the problem instead of the root of the problem. Usually when we argue with a spouse, parent, sibling, or close friend, the argument is not about the real problem. We argue about leaving a dirty dish on the table when the real problem is we feel our loved one intentionally or unintentionally hurt, disappointed, or offended us ten weeks ago. What I have found through research and personal experience is that debt is just a symptom of uncontrolled spending. Uncontrolled spending is the result of a lack of discipline. Lack of discipline is the result of lack of a proper relationship with the Father of all spirits through the saving grace of Jesus Christ and the revelation of the Holy Spirit. The mortgage mentality stems from a lack of relationship with the Holy Spirit. Our lack of relationship with the Holy Spirit is, in fact, the root of all debt. Let's examine Isa. 55:1-11 in pieces to hash this assertion out.

> *Isa. 55:1-2* "Ho, every one that thirsteth, come ye to the waters, and he that hath no money; come ye, buy, and eat; yea, come, buy wine and milk without money and without price. Wherefore do ye spend money for [that which is] not bread? and your labour for [that which] satisfieth not? hearken diligently unto me, and eat ye [that which is] good, and let your soul delight itself in fatness."

Water

The earth is made up of about 70 percent water. Your body is also made up of about 70 percent water. Water is essential to life. In this passage, the Lord is offering water to those who are thirsty. Better said, the Lord is offering up the essence of life to those who are void of life. Jesus describes it as living water (John 4:6-14). This living water is simply the Word of God. This is an open invitation to partake in the divine nature of God, which is life itself. Life represents an intimate connection or relationship with God. The absence of life, which is death, is merely a lack of relationship with God. Jesus proclaimed in John 14:6 that He is the way, the truth, and the life and no man could come to the Father except by Him. So we establish a relationship with the Father by accepting Jesus. The Spirit of God facilitates the relationship. The Holy Spirit (through Jeremiah) speaks of water like this in Jer. 2:13: "For my people have committed two evils; they have forsaken me the fountain of living waters, [and] hewed them out cisterns, broken cisterns, that can hold no water."

Without Money

The best part about this invite is that it only costs you time and effort. All you have to do is "come to the waters." Notice the additional goodies you can purchase without money: wine and milk. During this time in history and within this particular region, milk and wine were some of the most expensive products on the market. If you need a reference point for the value of the invitation to "come to the waters," then just use the most expensive natural goods you can find in the earth. So, not only will the Word of God promote life, but He will also give you access to the great spiritual and natural wealth needed to sustain life.

Resources and Effort

The Lord asks a question: Why are you spending your resources and effort on fruitless things and unproductive endeavors? Many of us are spending money and purportedly working hard, but we are still unfulfilled. Why is that? Many of us mistake that which sustains life (money) with He who is the source of life. We work and spend money to find wholeness, but money and a job cannot give us what they do not have the power to give.

Hearken, Eat and Delight in Fatness

Hearken deals with the notion of listening with the intent of obedience. The Lord obliges us to thoroughly listen with the intent of obedience. Immediately following the call to obedience, the Lord gives us tangible actions — eat that which is of God and allow your soul to delight in the abundance of the Lord. Your soul represents your personality. It is the real you that only you and God know. This is a personal relationship with God. Through steadfast obedience to the leading of the Spirit, the believer is in a position to allow his or her soul to experience the abundance of God. Again, this is a spiritual and natural abundance.

> *Isa.* **55:3-5** "Incline your ear, and come unto me: hear, and your soul shall live; and I will make an everlasting covenant with you, [even] the sure mercies of David. Behold, I have given him [for] a witness to the people, a leader and commander to the people. Behold, thou shalt call a nation [that] thou knowest not, and nations [that] knew thee not shall run unto thee because of the Lord thy God, and for the Holy One of Israel; for he hath glorified thee."

Incline and Come, Hear and Live

These verses again require action on the believer's part. *Incline* implies stretching or spreading out. *Hear* actually means to hear intelligently or hear with the intent of obedience. Obedience leads to life, which we have defined as having a proper relationship with the Father. Outside of obedience to the Word, there is no basis for relationship.

Witness, Leader, and Commander: Everlasting Covenant

This is expressly referring to Jesus Christ. He is the witness, the leader, and commander (Heb. 12:3). He represents the establishment of God's everlasting covenant with His children. It is through the Word of God that mankind is reunited with God. It is through the Spirit of God that mankind can fellowship with God.

> *Isa. 55:6-9* "Seek ye the Lord while he may be found, call ye upon him while he is near: Let the wicked forsake his way, and the unrighteous man his thoughts: and let him return unto the Lord, and he will have mercy upon him; and to our God, for he will abundantly pardon. For my thoughts [are] not your thoughts, neither [are] your ways my ways, saith the Lord. For [as] the heavens are higher than the earth, so are my ways higher than your ways, and my thoughts than your thoughts."

While

God will not continually compel mankind to take advantage of His invitation to reestablish a proper relationship with Him. In Rom. 1:28, Paul gives us an example of the Lord allowing people to think whatever they want to think when they are not willing to walk in the knowledge of God.

Wicked and Unrighteous

Isaiah is speaking to the people of God. He is talking to so-called believers. *Wicked* refers to actions against the truth of the gospel of Christ. *Unrighteous* refers to character flaws that misrepresent God. Wicked deals with not bearing the image of God (what others see) while unrighteous deals with misrepresenting the likeness of God (what you and God see). The call is to return to the Lord, which means to reflect the image and likeness of God as you were created to do.

Thoughts and Ways

After God declares through the prophet that His people should return to receive mercy and abundant pardons, He immediately cuts off the limited human mind by declaring that His thoughts and ways are not our thoughts and ways. Many of us cannot comprehend why God is willing to be so merciful and kind to us. God seeks to conquer that unhealthy pattern of thinking by basically saying, "Just trust Me on this one."

> *Isa. 55:10-11* "For as the rain cometh down, and the snow from heaven, and returneth not thither, but watereth the earth, and maketh it bring forth and bud, that it may give seed to the sower, and bread to the eater: So shall my word be that goeth forth out of my mouth: it shall not return unto me void, but it shall accomplish that which I please, and it shall prosper [in the thing] whereto I sent it."

Water Brings Forth

Here is the power of water again. Rain and snow water the earth. Because of this water, the earth becomes productive. The very purpose of the water is to ensure the earth can be productive. When the earth is productive it generates seeds and bread. Seeds are for investment. Bread is for consumption. More on that later.

The Word Accomplishes and Prospers

We now learn that water is a natural example of the Word of God. The Word (water) goes forth upon the hearts of men (earth) for the sole purpose of making mankind productive. The measure of productivity is twofold. One: it must accomplish the will or plan of God, not one's personal agenda. Two: it must result in abundance or prosperity. The Holy Spirit enacts the Word of God. It follows that for mankind to be productive again, they must develop an intimate relationship with the Spirit of God. This relationship works to demolish the root of debt. This relationship ushers in wholeness that kills the minimum payment mentality, crushes the monthly payment attitude, and destroys the inclination to keep up with the Joneses. At the same time, the Holy Spirit delivers peace and institutes direction and purpose.

Seeds for Your Soil

Debt Annihilation: Exod. 3:1-10, Isa. 14:24-27

1. What is God's reaction to debt (read: oppression)? How is that relevant to the believer today?

2. From Isa. 14:24-27, what can we safely conclude about the things that God purposes for His people? How does that help us as we approach debt?

Uncontrolled Spending:
Prov. 21:20, Prov. 29:3 and Prov. 22:26-27

1. According to Prov. 21:20, how does God refer to a person that spends all of his or her money? How do we go about changing that reputation?

2. According to Prov. 29:3, how important is it to your financial situation to be mindful of the company you keep?

3. Prov. 22:26-27 admonishes us to avoid spending money we do not have and signing for people who are spending money they do not have. Why is this important to maintaining a sound financial foundation?

Debt Release: Isaiah 55, Lev. 25:1-17 and 1 John 1 and 2

1. Isa. 55:1-7 invites us to a debt release party. The cost of the party is free from a financial perspective, but does cost us something. The cost: obedience. Why is obedience essential for the believer as it relates to remaining debt free?

2. In Isa. 55:8-13, we learn that the Word of God is foundational to prosperity. Why is that important for the believer to grasp and embrace?

3. In Lev. 25:1-12, what do we learn about the principal of planting and reaping? Who is the Source of all increase? Why is that important for the believer to understand?

4. In Lev. 25:13-17, what is God's attitude toward fair business practices and debt? How does this relate to the believer?

5. According to 1 John 1 and 2, Who is the Source of the believer's release from debt? And once made free from debt, Who teaches the believer to live debt free?

PART II

ATTITUDES, WORDS AND BEHAVIORS

*Mastering the Three Elements of
Financial Freedom*

CHAPTER 4

IT'S ALL ABOUT ATTITUDE

Why It Is Important to Lose Your Mind

In All Thy Ways

This chapter is not about the power of positive thinking. Positive thinking can only get you so far. The only real power is in the Holy Spirit and the thinking part is wrapped up in this question: What does God say about what I should be doing? This is the most crucial chapter of this book, so read it once and read it again. Then read it once more so it sticks.

> *2 Tim. 1:7* "For God hath not given us the spirit of fear; but of power, and of love, and of a sound mind."

Why is a sound mind important?

> *Prov. 23:7* "For as he (mankind) thinketh in his heart so [is] he: Eat and drink, saith he to thee; but his heart [is] not with thee."

This verse plainly tells us that what we think is who we are. If many of us took an inventory of what thoughts consume us daily, we would likely find we are not the person everyone thinks we are. In fact, we will certainly find we are not the person we, ourselves, think we are.

So why did God give us a mind if He knew we were going to be doing our own thing? Quite simply, God wants mankind to exercise the same power of choice He enjoys as the Creator of all things visible and invisible. He expects man to choose His methodology.

> *Prov. 3:5-6* "Trust in the Lord with all thine heart; and lean not into your own understanding. In all thy ways acknowledge him, and he shall direct thy paths."

This scripture is frequently quoted but seldom implemented. What God is saying is, "Believe Me and operate according to My system regardless of what you can see, feel, touch, taste, hear, and figure out. I set this world up and I know how to get you from Point A to Point B to Point C in the most efficient and effective manner. Trust Me. I created the money!"

"Acknowledge God" is not merely knowing God exists. James 2:19 reads, "Thou believest that there is one God; thou doest well: the devils also believe, and tremble." James writes this to the believer who knows about God, but is not living according to the Word of God. "Acknowledge God" implies an intimate relationship with God through the Spirit of God. It is talking about knowing what God already knows about the purpose for your life. One can only acknowledge God when one is committed to the works of God.

God First, Money Second...Why Is It so Hard?

> *Matt. 6:33* "...seek ye first the kingdom of God, and his righteousness; and all these things shall be added to you."

Prov. 10:22 "The blessing of the Lord, it maketh rich, and he addeth no sorrow with it."

When we begin to walk in kingdom principles and seek God for career direction, increase becomes a by-product of doing what we were created to do in the first place. Are you sorry you have to go to work? Then you may be missing "the blessing of the Lord" — the Holy Spirit. It is that internal guidance system that gets you where you need to be when you need to be there. Riches and things are the result of being led by the Spirit (that is, they follow after obedience). Riches and possessions are certainly available without "the blessing of the Lord." Just look around you. However, riches and possessions do not impress God (they are His anyway) and they definitely do not usher the presence of God into your life. Conversely, "the blessing of the Lord" encompasses all riches, both spiritual and natural.

Think on These Things

There is a direct link between God's thoughts and the believer's experience of abundance. Throughout scripture God equips man with the formula for true success and freedom: think like God thinks.

Josh. 1:8 "This book of the law shall not depart out of thy mouth; but thou shalt meditate therein day and night, that thou mayest observe to do according to all that is written therein: for then thou shalt make thy way prosperous, and then thou shalt have good success."

Ps. 1:1-3 "Blessed [is] the man that walketh not in the counsel of the ungodly, nor standeth in the way of sinners, nor sitteth in the seat of the scornful. But his delight [is] in the law of the Lord; and in his law doth he meditate day and night. And he shall be like a tree planted by the rivers of water, that bringeth forth his fruit in his season; his leaf also shall not wither; and whatsoever he doeth shall prosper."

1 Timothy 4:12, 15 "Let no man despise thy youth; but be thou an example of the believers, in word, in conversation, in charity, in spirit, in faith, in purity...Meditate upon these things; give thyself wholly to them; that thy profiting may appear to all."

These three passages admonish us to meditate on the Word of God.

Meditate
This is the Hebrew word *hagah* (haw-gaw') and the Greek word *meletao* (mel-et-ah'-o). It means to ponder or revolve in the mind. This is a continual, persistent effort.

The Word of God
Why is God cautioning us to meditate on His Word? A word is simply a revealed thought. So God is saying, "If you want to know what I think, think about My Word." If you are wondering what God thinks about you and what you should be doing with money, meditate on His Word. It tells you exactly what He thinks.

Result of Meditation
Many of us are searching for success and prosperity. In fact, many of us have probably achieved some level of success and prosperity in our lives. Many of us are still searching for that ultimate success. That ultimate success is tied up in the Word of God. Examine the words and phrases associated with meditation in God's Word — "prosperous," "good success," "fruit," "shall not wither," and "profit-

ing may appear." These powerful concepts imply that great achievement results from meditation on the will of God.

How Should I Think About Money?

The principal reason people cannot get their financial house in order is because they do not truly embrace what money is. Therefore they cannot get to a place in their mind where they can acknowledge God in that area of their life. They do not meditate on what the Word of God says about money. We learned in chapter 2 that money is merely a resource. Let's dig deeper to discover what a resource really is.

A *resource* is the entire means available for the purpose of productivity and/or maturity. The resource represents the whole amount available. The resource can do nothing in and of itself. The resource is typically not owned by the resource-user. The resource serves a distinct purpose — production and/or maturity.

The earth was created to work for us (Gen. 1:29). We were not created to spend our entire life working for money. We were created to manipulate resources to do what God designed us to do, which is to be productive in the earth. Resources are supposed to sustain us, not be our ultimate goal in life. Is that how you think about money? Be honest!

God's Attitude about Money and Success

Ps. 35:27 "Let them shout for joy, and be glad, that favour my righteous cause: yea, let them say continually, Let the Lord be magnified, which hath pleasure in the prosperity of his servant."

Righteous Cause

How many people know living as an example of God in the earth realm is a righteous cause? How many people know it is an awesome calling and brings unspeakable satisfaction? How many people know it is a source of joy and gladness? How many people know when people see you they should see God? That's how God is magnified and given glory. This is a 24/7 experience.

God's Delight

David boldly suggests we should be continuously aware that God has pleasure in the prosperity of his servant. In Merriam Webster's Collegiate Dictionary the first definition of the word *pleasure* is desire or inclination. Another definition is a state of gratification. That word *gratification* is related to the word *satisfaction*. Satisfaction can be associated with the word complete. So what are we working with? God gets a sense of wholeness when his people are prosperous. (Please don't misunderstand me. God does not need you to be rich for Him to be whole and complete.) God's desire and inclination is for the people of God to be prosperous — this is a source of satisfaction for Him!

Let us think about why this would be. Well, did God create man? Have we learned what image and likeness God created man in? Have we learned what God created man for? Do we need a refresher? God created man to experience his divine nature and abundant riches. Why would He not receive satisfaction in seeing you successful and prosperous?

Prosperity

This is the condition of being successful or thriving, especially economic well-being.

Let's work with the word *success*. *Success* means outcome or result. We can alter that to mean purpose or fruit. We can also associate it with the word destiny. Dr. Myles Munroe said something profound in a teaching on "The Power of Personal Destiny." He said (and I'm paraphrasing) true success only comes when you are doing what God created you to do.

Let me see if I can get us there. Prosperity is about success. Success is about results. Results are about bearing fruit. It follows that prosperity is tied up in bearing fruit.

> *John 15:16* "Ye have not chosen me, but I have chosen you, and ordained (empowered, anointed, blessed) you, that you should go and bring forth fruit (results, success), and [that] your fruit should remain..."

God had a specific purpose in mind when He sent you into the earth at this time. This purpose is your result. It is your fruit. It is your measure of success. Anything other than that falls short of success. The success (or desired outcome) God has put before you is so powerful it will cause you to bear fruit both naturally and spiritually (Gal. 5:22-24), lead you to natural prosperity, and extend beyond your generation into generations to come (John 15:16).

The Mindset of Stewardship

How does God expect us to handle the money resource? What should be our mental approach to money? God has very specific principles in His Word related to money management. This takes us back to our key word: *resource*. If you are an employee, you are a steward. You get paid to manage the resources of someone else. By the same token, God gave mankind stewardship over all the resources of the earth. Those resources exist so mankind can live off the abundance God purposely put in the earth. The earth is one big resource. The way we lay claim to pieces of that resource is with money. The process works like this: Man plants and waters the resources and God causes the resources to expand exponentially. Now if man decides to consume the resources, then the entire expansion process is cut off — not only for that individual, but for every individual that was depending on that individual, and every individual that was depending on those individuals, and so forth. Does anybody wonder why generations of people continue to wallow in poverty and lack?

Matt. 25:14-30 and Luke 19:12-27 detail the story of a man giving his servants stewardship over his goods. In this instance, the servants received what they could handle given their ability. (This parable is discussed in detail in *Start Planting!*). What we want to spend time on is the result of this stewardship project. The two servants who planted and watered the resources were rewarded with great gain. The one servant who ate or consumed the seed, or basically did not put it to its intended use, did not see any increase and was berated before being cast into outer darkness for his lack of profitability.

So what's the moral of the story? The purpose of money is for mankind to use money to be profitable in life. What does that mean? When we talk about being profitable, we are talking about being successful. True success only comes from doing what God created you to do. In that success is peace, joy, happiness, and wouldn't you know it — money! The most important attitude to embrace about money is this: it is not yours! It belongs to God and you are supposed to manage it. In order to successfully manage it, you have to learn how it works!

Why Should I Adopt the Mindset of Stewardship?

The basic answer is because that is what God originally created you to do. Nevertheless, as always, we have to take it to the scriptures. Luke 16:1-9 speaks of a certain rich man who had an unjust steward (man turned digger) who was accused of wasting the rich man's goods. The rich man summoned the steward and told him to explain himself. Shortly thereafter, the rich man fired the steward. Now the steward was stuck because he had embraced a lifestyle of doing that which he was not hired to do — operating as a digger. He quickly devised a plan to essentially do the job he should have been doing in the first place — taking care of the rich man's money. He called up every last one of the rich man's debtors and put them on a collection plan that included forgiving some of the debt they owed. As a result, he returned some money to the rich man and now had friends all over the land because the rich man's debtors were happy to be debt free. They obviously could not afford to pay the rich man yet they were able to make a partial payment and be released from the slavery of debt through the wise planning of the unjust steward. A funny thing happened after that. Let's read.

> *Luke 16:8-9* "And the lord commended the unjust steward, because he had done wisely: for the children of this world are in their generation wiser than the children of light. And I say unto you, Make to yourselves friends of the mammon of unrighteousness; that, when ye fail, they may receive you into everlasting habitations."

Unjust Steward

This phrase is synonymous with the term we have coined throughout this project: digger. Please notice that just because the "steward" performed wisely he did not lose the title of "unjust." He clearly exhibited the digger mentality.

Wiser Generation

It amazes me this parable was given over two thousand years ago and is still undoubtedly relevant to modern day children of light. Many believers are so "Christian" they miss the practical principles of commerce. The digger understood he operated in a world that is full of money. He realized he had something in common with both his former boss and the folks that owed his former boss — they all need money. He then put on his natural, God-given thinking cap and devised a scheme to appease all parties involved. Notice he did not get on his knees and pray for some money or a job to fall out of the sky. He formulated a plan and worked it to perfection!

Make Friends of the Mammon of Unrighteousness

This passage has always intrigued me (okay...so it really, really bothered me) so I prayed and prayed for better revelation. Are you ready? Jesus encourages believers to make friends with those who possess wealth accumulated outside of the will of God (the mammon of unrighteousness). Jesus goes on to say we should do this "that when you may fail they may receive you into everlasting habitations." Now, I have to be honest. This never made one bit of sense to me. How are the folks with the mammon of unrighteousness going to receive me into everlasting habitations? What do they possess that lasts forever? The answer is nothing! Watch the awesomeness of God!

In the original Greek translation of the New Testament, a couple of words are noticeably absent from verse nine — *that* and *they*. And the word *fail* actually means "die." The phrase actually should read, "Make friends of the mammon of unrighteousness; whenever you die you will be received into a perpetual tabernacle." Are you still with me? People with the mammon of unrighteousness do not have an everlasting tabernacle to receive us into. Only God can receive us into an everlasting dwelling place. See, the purpose of the children of light is to literally be a light. We are to exercise influence and shine our light in the darkness — among the mammon of unrighteousness. When this is done, it should be no surprise that we would eventually be received into an everlasting habitation by God. On top of that, our light becomes an attraction to our lost brothers and sisters. We become a living example to them of how to approach life and the money resource. We are in a position to save souls. This is why Jesus recommends we make friends! It is the wise thing to do (Prov. 11:30).

The Mindset of Giving

In 2 Corinthians 9, Paul is writing to the church at Corinth and he is talking about giving to the ministry.

> *2 Cor. 9:6-8,11* "...He which soweth sparingly shall reap also sparingly; and he which soweth bountifully shall reap also bountifully. Every man according as he purposeth in his heart, [so let him give]; not grudgingly, or of necessity: for God loveth a cheerful giver. And God [is] able to make all grace abound toward you; that ye, always having all sufficiency in all [things], may abound to every good (read: God-inspired, not self-inspired) work...Being enriched in every thing to all bountifulness, which causeth through us thanksgiving to God."

Sow and Reap

This is a universal principle. I am sure you have heard the phrase "what goes around, comes around" plenty of times. That is man's version of God's sow and reap principle. God has placed physical examples all around us. If you sow an apple seed, you reap apples off an apple tree. You sow the seed; you cultivate it; you have absolutely no control over how it grows; you wait for the tree's season; you pick the apples; you eat the apples; and you repeat the cycle. You cannot plant apple seeds and get oranges. Or, think of it this way: if you give small, you get small. It is irrational to think otherwise.

As He Purposeth in his Heart

This is where some people are stuck. God is concerned about how you give, not how much. Do we really give our best or do we give just to be giving something? Do we approach giving with the proper attitude?

God Is Able

This is an awesome passage! Paul is talking about giving and how to give with a cheerful heart. Then he says "and (i.e., when you give with a cheerful heart) God is able." This is essentially saying your giving is what makes God able. Able to do what? "To make all grace abound toward you." What is grace? At Look Up and Live Ministries, we define *grace* as God's power, knowledge, wisdom, and ability at man's disposal. So when you give cheerfully, you gain access to God's omnipotent power. The flipside is that when you do not give cheerfully you are shut off from the power of God. Somebody say, Amen!

Having All Sufficiency in All Things

These verses tell us that God wants us to be rich in all areas of life: spiritually, mentally, physically, and financially. The verses say "always," "all sufficiency," "all things," "every thing," and "all bountifulness." Does that leave anything out? He wants you to have all of those resources to do what he called you to do and so others can see you and glorify Him. It does not sound like mankind should be struggling to pay some monthly bills.

So when we tie this thing together, we see that what you receive is directly related to how you give. See, we have access to the grace of God, but the way we give is what limits how much of the grace we can walk in. The scripture plainly says, "God is able to make all grace abound toward you." So He has the ability and wants all grace to abound toward you, but you have to give Him something to work with.

A Tithing Myth Revealed

Many Christians have been taught they should tithe and give offerings so God can give them some money back thirty-, sixty-, and hundred-fold. This is not the proper mindset to have about giving money. First, let's go to the source of this myth. It is found in the parable of the sower (Matthew 13, Mark 4 and Luke 8). This parable speaks about the Word of God bringing forth the fruit of the Spirit (Gal. 5:22-23) in a believer's life "thirty-, sixty-, and a hundred-fold." People continue to teach the parable in the context of money and it has absolutely nothing to do with money. Tithing has absolutely nothing to do with getting some money from God thirty-, sixty-, and a hundred-fold. The way you get money is by working!

Now that we have destroyed that myth, let's take a look at the tithe. A tithe is a tenth. The traditional text for this topic is Mal. 3:6-12. Let's work with some of the verses. Mal. 3:8-9 starts off with the phrase, "Will a man rob God?" That sounds so intimidating. Is that supposed to scare somebody? That's exactly how preachers use it! In Young's Literal Translation of the Bible, that passage reads, "Doth man deceive God? but ye are deceiving Me, And ye have said: 'In what have we deceived Thee?' The tithe and the heave-offering."

When reading the Bible, we should always look at the context in which statements are made. Prior to this particular passage, Malachi is essentially preaching to the Levites, who were the priests, about their unsatisfactory performance. One thing that was unsatisfactory about their behavior is they were violating the Mosaic law of tithing. Not only were they violating the law, the entire nation was too.

As it is used in the Malachi passage, the word *deceive* means to cheat. So why would God say the Levites and the children of Israel were cheating Him? Lev. 27:30 states, "And all the tithe of the land, [whether] of the seed of the land, [or] of the fruit of the tree (recall: money grows on trees), [is] the Lord's: [it is] holy unto the Lord." In this context, *holy* means devoted entirely. In other words, the tithe legally belonged to God, not to the people of God.

Mal. 3:10 (Young's Literal Translation) goes on to say, "Bring in all the tithe unto the treasure-house, And there is food in My house; When ye have tried Me, now, with this, Said Jehovah of Hosts, Do not I open to you the windows of heaven?" Now I have to credit John Cherry and his son, John Cherry II, for giving me some deep insight on this. Here's the one-second version. There is no money in the windows of heaven. The tithe was used to take care of the business of ministry.

Beyond Tithing — the Mindset of Giving

The verses we've examined about tithing come out of the Old Testament law. In the eighth chapter of Hebrews, Paul, through the guidance of the Holy Spirit, beautifully contrasts the Old Testament law with the ministry of Jesus Christ. In that chapter and throughout Hebrews, we find the law was a shadow or example of the standard that the death and resurrection of Jesus the Christ would bring back to mankind. Jesus declares in Matt. 6:17 that He came to fulfill the law, meaning, "I've got something better for you." God was not so much concerned about the tithe as He was about truly adopting the mindset of giving. In fact, the legalism of tithing is not mentioned after the resurrection of Jesus Christ.

The tithe is only 10 percent. It is such a menial amount. It is so basic. It legally belongs to God as everything does. The tithe is so elementary that it should not even be an issue with a Christian. When the Holy Spirit stepped on the scene in the book of Acts, believers over and over again sold their possessions, put their money in the ministry, and took freely from the pot as they had need (Acts 2:45, 4:35). In other words, they gave 100 percent, fully expecting to be taken care of by the work of the ministry! Tithing is old news!

Don't get me wrong. Tithing is a great starting point that will foster discipline and unleash some spiritual blessings. But it by no means should be the focus of a believer's giving. Even in the Old Testament they gave more than just a tithe. There were various offerings. Giving takes many forms. It is not limited to dropping some money in the offering basket every week. You can sow money into people's lives. You can minister to other people's financial needs.

When you adopt a mindset of giving, God gives you spiritual insights to dominate your personal situations. Without it, we can end up cheating God because He cannot endow us with the spiritual blessings that will lead to great success and prosperity in the earth realm. He created us to pour out His spiritual power upon us and to dwell with us. But when we reject His mindset of giving, we are shut off from our purpose — we are useless. In essence, the windows of heaven are shut closed!

The Mindset of Giving on Display

Let's look at this concept of giving by examining a familiar story. Remember when the wise men visited Jesus? Watch this! It is likely that there were more than three wise men. We need to lay that Christmas story to rest. There were three types of gifts, but the Bible never says there were three wise men. If we study out the wise men, we will find they did not travel in mere packs of threes. Furthermore, when we read the story closely, we see that these wise men must have been some large attraction since King Herod noticed them and asked to meet with them (Matt. 2:7). Now to the juicy part...what happened when this group of wise men showed up to see the young child Jesus in Mary and Joseph's house. First, they worshipped Him. Then they gave Him money! Please do not miss the order of events. The Bible says in Matt. 2:11 that they "opened their treasures." Why did they give Him money? Did anyone read the dissertation on tithes and offerings above? The money gifts of the wise men "opened up the windows of heaven" and gave God the right to empower the ministry of Jesus Christ. That money represented a natural seed into the ministry of Jesus that released the spiritual blessings of God into His life and into the lives of the wise men. The spiritual power unleashed by the wise men's gifts continues to pay dividends today as we are beneficiaries of the ministry of Jesus Christ. They did not drop the money in the offering plate. They sowed it into His life.

The purpose of giving is to unleash the awesome power of the Spirit of God in your life and others. God is not trying to scare us into giving Him money. He does not need it. What is He going to do with it? He created the money. He is trying to show us the spiritual principal of sowing and reaping. When we give God our best, He is obligated to give us His best. From a natural standpoint, if we are honest with ourselves, we place the most value on money. How many people know God's best is better than what we consider to be best? How many people know if you give small you get small?

> *Luke 6:38* "Give, and it shall be given unto you; good measure, pressed down, and shaken together, and running over, shall men give into your bosom. For with the same measure that ye mete withal it shall be measured to you again."

Spiritual In-Sight or Natural Out-Sight?
Why does Jesus only identify two masters in Matt. 6:24, neither of whom are the Devil? A *master* is one supreme in authority or one in control. The two masters identified as the ones that would rule a living soul's life are money and God. The former is a natural god and the latter is a spiritual god. Realize there is absolutely no way to serve both authorities. Until now we have hinted around this point: **The whole earth is literally money.** This is a life-altering revelation, so don't miss it.

All you do and all you live revolve around the earth. It permeates the natural eyes. It demands your attention and focus. Just before the statement about masters, Jesus describes the natural eye as the light of the whole body (Matt. 6:22-23). Watch this...how many people know there are natural eyes and spiritual eyes? How many people know the natural eyes (external) and the spiritual eyes (internal) do not see the same things? Don't miss the revelation of the Spirit.

With your natural eye you see all that is in the earth — wealth, abundance, and splendor. You observe the magnificence of the earth's great riches. You desire to partake in those riches. Your actions are determined by what you see with your natural eyes. Your whole existence becomes about making money for the sole purpose of participating in that which you see and like — the earth. You offer your talents, abilities, and effort to collect a paycheck that will allow you to claim pieces of the earth. The earth subtly becomes the object of your affection. You soon have no vision beyond the external. Your out-sight is in full swing. You have to eat. You have to drink. You have to be merry. That's what life is all about. Right?

To contrast this, the Bible describes the spirit of the man as the candle (light) of the Lord (Prov. 20:27). The Spirit provides in-sight. Paul clues us in to this phenomenon in Gal. 6:17, which says the flesh (the natural eye) is contrary to the Spirit (the spiritual eye). The only way to communicate with God is in the spirit. Jesus said something very peculiar during His earthly ministry. Over and over He said He came to open the blind eyes, but the kicker is He was talking to people that could naturally see. So what blind eyes did he come to open? Well, the digger mentality ushered in by the Adams results in spiritual blindness. In other words, you cannot even see who you really are. Remember, the Adams merely relied on the earth instead of the Holy Spirit. Jesus came to reestablish a spiritual connection between God and mankind (i.e., to open the blind eyes). In the book of John, Jesus asserts that the time has come for true worshippers to worship God in spirit and in truth. Well what is worship? There are many ways to worship, but we can sum it up like this: Respect the authority of the Spirit of God! Worship is about reverence and obedience. Worship implies a proper relationship with God. What is that relationship? Trust in the Lord with all your heart and lean not unto your own understanding (your out-sight). In other words, meditate on the Word of God.

My New Attitude about Money

The money issue is a matter of focus. Focus comes from the eyes. Eyes are what allow vision. It is impractical to follow two visions. As my pastor eloquently puts it, two visions are where we get the word *di-vision*. In other words, we are not all one with the plan and purpose of God. The conclusion to the whole matter is that God wants our focus to be on the Creator, not the created. The Creator holds the vision. The created is merely a resource in the vision. Since folks keep treating the created as the actual vision, people remain confused and unfulfilled. If your vision only revolves around figuring out how to obtain as much of the stuff you see around you as fast as humanly possible (external), you will miss the plan and purpose of God (internal). You may have noticed we are dealing with the sixth chapter of Matthew backwards. Let us continue...

> *Matt. 6:19-21* "Lay not up for yourselves treasures upon earth, where moth and rust doth corrupt, and where thieves break through and steal: But lay up for your-selves treasures in heaven, where neither moth nor rust doth corrupt, and where thieves do not break through nor steal: For where your treasure is, there will your heart be also."

This book is about money, but this passage in Matthew seems to imply we should just ignore money. I would argue this passage says no such thing. This passage is about focus.

Proper Context

Remember these verses directly precede verses 22 and 23, which talk about the natural eye being the light of the whole body. According-ly, we can conclude that laying up treasures is about focus (i.e., what you are concentrating on). So what is your focus? Verse 21 says that when I see what you are focused on, I know exactly what is on your mind. So you can tell me all day that money is not your focus, but when everything you do is based on money and natural things your focus is evident. The only person you have fooled is yourself.

Treasure

That word *treasure* is literally talking about a deposit. When we think of the word *deposit* we think of the word *bank*. What do we store in a bank? How many people say money or wealth? But what God is trying to show us is that this earth is just a replica or shadow of the true riches of God, which are in Christ Jesus. The true riches are spir-itual. The true riches come from the windows of heaven. The pas-sage merely advises us to focus on the spiritual wealth of the Father because the natural wealth is temporary. By all means, enjoy the nat-ural wealth that is the earth, but focus on the purpose and plan of God. In fact, the spiritual wealth of God leads to natural wealth in the earth.

In Col. 3:1-2, Paul admonishes us to focus on heavenly things. What are those heavenly things?

> *Matt. 6:33* "Seek ye first the kingdom of God, and His righteousness; and all these things (the earth) will be added to you.

The Kingdom of God

A kingdom is a place where the king has domain. In other words, what the king says goes! Luke 17:20-21 reads as follows, "And when he (Jesus) was demanded of the Pharisees, when the kingdom of God should come, he answered them and said, The kingdom of God cometh not with observation: Neither shall they say, Lo here! or, lo there! for, behold, the kingdom of God is within you."

Let's piece it together. If a kingdom is a place where the king has domain and the kingdom of God is within mankind, then the kingdom of God must be the amount of influence the Holy Spirit has in a believer's life. So the scripture is telling us to seek the counsel of the Holy Spirit before we do anything. How profound is that? God is saying to seek His counsel before you decide what careers you want to pursue. Before you decide what to do with your money, seek His counsel. Before you decide to get married, seek His counsel. So the first focus we must embrace is that of seeking the counsel of the Holy Spirit—before we act! This leads us to think like God, which is the focus of this chapter.

His Righteousness

In conjunction with seeking the counsel of the Holy Spirit, Jesus tells us to seek the righteousness of God. Understand that as believers we have indeed been made the righteousness of God (2 Cor. 5:21). Having received the divine nature of God, we are expected to exhibit the righteousness of God. So what is "His righteousness?" This deliberately refers to the very character of God. It speaks to the very way God acts. It speaks to exhibiting the fruit of the Spirit — love, joy, peace, longsuffering, gentleness, goodness, faith, meekness, and temperance. So our second focus must be that of seeking to act like God.

Added Things

We were built and created to operate in and inhabit the earth. What do we need to effectively fulfill that purpose? Say it with me people: Money! Remember the earth is money. It is the inheritance of mankind. Once we have properly linked up with the Source of the earth ("these things") then money becomes a by-product of following God. So our third focus must be that of establishing the proper order in our lives. Money is not the principal thing — wisdom or the Word of God is (Prov. 4:7). The Holy Spirit counsels us according to the Word of God. Money is the resource that helps us fulfill that which God gives us to accomplish.

Seeds for Your Soil

Trust in God: 2 Timothy 1 and Proverbs 3

1. According to 2 Tim. 1:7, what kind of spirit does the believer have? How does knowing that facilitate trust in God?

2. According to Proverbs 3, what types of things result in the believer's life when he or she trusts in God? Make a list.

The Mind of Christ:
Josh. 1:1-8, Psalm 1, 1 Timothy 4, and Philippians 2

1. Josh. 1:1-8 gives us some keys to success and prosperity. Psalm 1 echoes the sentiment. The same concept is reinforced by 1 Tim. 4:15-16. What does it really mean to meditate on the Word of God day and night?

2. According to Philippians 2, what things make up the mind of Christ and why is it important for the believer to allow the mind of Christ to be in him or her?

Stewardship Mentality:
Matt. 25:14-30, Luke 19:12-27, and Luke 16:1-13

1. List three things you learn from reading Matt. 25:14-30 and Luke 19:12-27.

2. Based on your reading of Luke 16:1-13, list three characteristics that manifest in a person's life as the result of having a stewardship mentality.

The Giver's Mentality:
2 Corinthians 9, Malachi 3, and Acts 1 and 2

1. What can we learn about the principle of planting and reaping after reading 2 Corinthians 9?

2. List the results of giving tithes and offerings to the service of the kingdom of God as described in Malachi 3.

3. Describe how God's gift of the Holy Spirit to the believer operated and affected people's lives in Acts 1 and 2.

The Believer's Winning Attitude:
Matt. 6:19-34 and Colossians 3:1-17

1. Name three specific things we learn in Matt. 6:19-34 about God's attitude toward the material resources that He created for us to enjoy in the first place. How then should we approach material resources?

2. According to Col. 3:1-17, what should the believer's focus be on and what specific things should the believer concentrate his or her daily efforts on?

CHAPTER 5

SHUT UP!

Why My Biggest Enemy Is My Own Mouth

And God Said...and There Was

Now that we have the mindset of stewardship and giving, we are positioned to speak life into our finances. Words are the source of the worlds, the source of 100 percent of our successes, and the source of 100 percent of our problems. We take words for granted, but they are the very source of our existence. God established order in the earth like this: (1) God thought about what He wanted; (2) God spoke His plan; (3) The Spirit of God brought what God had purposed in His heart into existence.

> *Gen. 1:26* "And God said, Let us make man in our image, after our likeness..."

Did anybody notice the phrase "And God said"? We were designed to operate in the same manner. Think! Speak! Things come into existence! Words are the only thing that make things happen in the earth realm — good or bad.

A Matter of Life or Death...Literally

> *Prov. 18:21* "Death and life are in the power of the tongue: and they that love it shall eat the fruit thereof."

Remember that saying: Sticks and stones may break my bones, but words will never hurt me? Who thinks that statement is true? How many of us know that words can cut you deeply and stay with you for a while? How many people know that only God can heal the pain you feel? This is because words are spiritual seeds that can result in spiritual wounds, which can grow over time into full-grown fruit. Let us think about the preceding verse.

Death and Life

We speak one of two things when we open our mouths — things that line up with the Word of God or things that do not line up with the Word of God. Life is in the former and death is in the latter. What do we mean? Our mouth is the gateway to developing a relationship with God or spiritually separating ourselves from God. Every time we say anything, we are planting seeds (sowing) in the spiritual realm.

Gal. 6:7-8 reads, "Be not deceived (run amuck; led astray; hoodwinked; bamboozled); God is not mocked (disregarded): for whatsoever (all things) a man soweth (speaks), that (the thing that he/she sows) shall (100 percent) he also reap. For he that soweth to his flesh (speaks according to feelings, emotions, will, intellect) shall (100 percent) of the flesh (expect someone to hurt your feelings, play with your emotions, act selfishly toward you, and so forth) reap corruption (death, separation from God); but he that soweth to the Spirit (speaks according to the Word of God as taught by the Holy Spirit) shall of the Spirit reap life everlasting." There is no variation in this spiritual law. This definitely happens every time we open our mouths, whether we believe God or not.

The Power of the Tongue

That word *power* is the Hebrew word *koach* (ko'-akh), which is defined as an ability to do something. The dictionary defines *power* as possession of control, authority, or influence. Now let's finish Gen. 1:26. "..and let them have dominion (supreme authority)...over all the earth..." Are you following me? God made us in His image and after His likeness so the authority we have been given in the earth is manifested through our mouths. Nothing moves in the earth or natural realm without the permission of a man or woman. This permission is granted verbally, every time we speak.

They that Love It Shall Eat the Fruit Thereof

Speaking of "they that love it," God is talking about those who always have to get the last word in or give someone a piece of their mind. God is good. He gives us natural examples to illustrate spiritual principles.

Seeds grow into fruit and growing fruit is not an overnight process. God tells us we will absolutely eat the fruit we plant! Not only that, but seeds we have planted may grow up three years down the line, eight years down the line, or fifteen years down the line. Only God knows. Furthermore, God is the only one who sets the consequences for our words. So while we can choose what to say, we cannot choose the result. This is why we must speak according to the Word of God. The Word illustrates the benefits of saying what God says and it also points out the consequences of doing the opposite.

Power of Words

Let's run down some scriptures that address the power of words.

Prov. 15:4 "A wholesome tongue [is] a tree of life: but perverseness (words against the Word of God) therein [is] a breach (violation) in the spirit."

Prov. 10:11 "The mouth of a righteous [man is] a well of life: but violence covereth the mouth of the wicked."

Prov. 16:23-24 "The heart (mind or thought life) of the wise teacheth his mouth, and addeth learning to his lips. Pleasant words [are]...sweet to the soul and health to the bones (body)."

Matt. 12:33-37 "Either make the tree good, and his fruit good; or else make the tree corrupt...for the tree is known by [his] fruit...for out of the abundance of the heart (thoughts; meditation) the mouth speaketh. A good man out of the good treasure (the Word of God) of the heart bringeth forth good things: and an evil man out of the evil treasure (against the Word of God) of his heart bringeth forth evil things. But I say unto you, That every idle word that men shall speak, they shall give account for in the day of judgment. For by thy words thou shalt be justified, and by thy words thou shalt be condemned."

Prov. 4:23-24 "Keep thy heart with all diligence; for out of it [are] the issues of life. Put away from thee a froward (disobedient) mouth, and perverse (against the Word of God) lips put far from thee."

James 1:19 "...let every man be swift to hear, slow to speak, slow to wrath."

Ps. 5:1, 3 "Give ear to my words, O Lord, consider my meditation...My voice shalt thou hear in the morning..."

Prov. 18:20 "A man's belly shall be satisfied with the fruit of his mouth; [and] with the increase of his lips shall he be filled."

Many of us get upset when adverse things happen to us and we blame God for them. We also blame other people. The reality of the matter is something is wrong with us. There is nothing wrong with God or other people. There is something wrong with what we think and say about God, about other people, and about our situations and circumstances.

Prov. 13:3 "He that keepeth his mouth keepeth his life: but he that openeth wide his lips shall have destruction."

Keep
The very first definition of *keep* is to take notice by appropriate conduct. Let me put it in laymen's terms: some things you should say; some things you should not.

Shall Have
Again, no man controls this consequence. God said it! This is a 100 percent guarantee.

Destruction
This is the condition of being useless or ineffective. Enough said.

It sounds to me like the words we speak dictate the quality of life we live. Many of us frequently speak uselessness and ineffectiveness into our own lives. It is because we do not know any better. We already talked about people being destroyed for lack of knowledge. What things do you say on a daily basis concerning the money resource?

Exposing the Tongue

James 3:2, 5-6, 8-10 "...If any man offend not in word, the same [is] a perfect man, [and] able also to bridle the whole body...the tongue is a little member, and boasteth great things. Behold, how great a matter a little fire kindleth! And the tongue [is] a fire, a world of iniquity...it defileth the whole body, and setteth on fire the course of nature; and it is set on fire of hell...the tongue can no man tame; [it is] an unruly evil, full of deadly poison. Therewith bless we God, even the Father; and therewith curse we men, which are made after the similitude of God. Out of the same mouth proceedeth blessing and cursing. My brethren, these things ought not so to be."

Perfect Man

This is talking about a mature male or female living soul. This mature person is able, through the proper use of words, to control his actions and reactions.

Little Fire

How many people know it doesn't take long for a little fire to turn into a big fire? The passage suggests the misused tongue dishonors the whole body. This results in improper actions, reactions, and a mess bigger than you could have ever conceived.

Nature and Hell

What is more interesting is it says, "...setteth on fire the course of nature; and it (meaning nature) is set on the fire of hell..." This is a rich teaching. Hell was never intended for mankind (see Matt. 25:41 and Isa. 5:13-14) and never meant for the natural realm. Men and women literally speak hell into the earth. I hope somebody heard that. The unbridled tongue is what brings hell to earth. Lack of knowledge about what to say concerning your life's situations and circumstances (this includes finances) is making your life a living hell.

No Man Can Tame

How many times have we intended to say the right thing, but it did not quite turn out right? It takes supernatural power to get your mouth under control. We need the power of the Holy Spirit within us to bridle our tongues.

Unruly Evil

Unruly means not readily ruled, disciplined, or managed. *Evil* means completely opposite of God. Enough said.

Blessing and Cursing

Deut. 30:19 says, "I call heaven and earth to record this day against you, [that] I have set before you life and death, blessing and cursing: therefore choose life, that both thou and thy seed may live." We choose to speak life or death (Prov. 18:21) every time we open our mouths. Life indicates an eternal relationship with the Father and death means separation from the Father, for which the end result is hell. Many will experience hell in the earth and receive the real thing at their natural death.

Similitude of God

Consider these two phrases: "in His image" and "after His likeness."

In other words, would God talk to you like that and would you talk to God like that? What does God say about your finances?

Who knew the tongue did all that?

Corrupt Communication

> *Eph. 4:29-30* "Let no corrupt communication proceed out of your mouth, but that which is good to the use of edifying, that it may minister grace unto the hearers. And grieve not the Holy Spirit of God, whereby ye are sealed unto the day of redemption."

Corrupt Communication

Corrupt means altered from the original or correct form or version. *Communication* is a process by which information is exchanged. So *corrupt communication* is an information exchange that is not functioning according to its proper or correct purpose. This portion of the passage is basically saying, "Don't exchange any information outside of God's purpose!" One of God's purposes is for mankind to live abundantly right now in the earth.

Use of Edifying

The word *edify* means to build, establish, instruct, or improve. If our words are not doing those things, they are not being spoken according to God's purpose.

Grieving the Holy Spirit

God is literally saddened when we speak things that are out of line with His will. I would suggest He is saddened because He knows the end of those things spoken inside His will as well as the end of those things that are spoken out of order.

Words are spiritual. Each comment that comes out of our mouths sets off activity in the spirit realm. This is a powerful lesson. God created the worlds with His Word. Those same creative powers lie within our mouths. Things that are happening to and around us are the result of what we have been speaking and what we have allowed others to speak into our lives.

Stop Saying Dumb Stuff!

There is a bevy of famous last words we speak concerning our finances:

"I'm broke!"

"I could never afford that!"

"I will just charge it now and pay it off later!"

"We will never have enough money for that!"

"I don't make enough money to tithe!"

"I don't make enough money to save!"

"I can't pay my bills!"

Sometimes we just need to shut up. Many people are in a financial bind because of their mouths — literally unleashing the fire of hell throughout your bank account! We have to learn to say what God says concerning our resources. First and foremost, God gave us dominion over all the resources of the earth. Dominion manifests in our mouths. We must exercise control over our resources with what we say. Second, to properly exercise control, we must know what the Word says concerning the money resource. In chapter 2, we defined money and put it in its proper perspective as a resource. In the previous chapter, we talked about how we should think about money — from a perspective of stewardship and from a perspective of giving. Our communication concerning money should reflect the attitude of God.

What do our famous last words look like when we adopt the mind of Christ and speak the Word of God?

❧ Father, your Word proclaims you created me in your image

and after your likeness. Not only that, you gave me dominion over all of your natural wealth and access to all of your spiritual wealth. I am wealthy and am depending on you to lead me into my wealthy place.

❧ The earth is the Lord's and the fullness thereof! I praise God for endowing me with the ideas and bringing me before the contacts I need to generate the resources required for everything I need to fulfill His purpose for my life.

❧ I owe no man anything but love. I thank God for the discipline to save until I can afford this item. I thank God for ideas to generate additional sources of income so I don't have to spend as much time saving.

❧ I magnify your name Lord for it is you who gives me the power to lay claim to pieces of the earth. I praise you because I know that promotion comes neither from the east nor the west, but it comes from you. It is a blessing to know you are a God of increase and you are exceedingly able to produce increase in my financial resources.

❧ Father, it is only reasonable I dedicate a portion of my revenues to Your earthly ministry as You seek to reunite with your sons. You declare in your Word that my giving unleashes spiritual power and protects my natural assets so I am firmly standing on that Word.

❧ Lord, You say the laborer is worthy of his wages so there is no way I am going to work every day and not have enough to set aside for myself. You created me to live in abundance and I am storing up resources every time I make money.

• I have more than enough resources to meet my monthly obligations because my God supplies all my needs according to His riches in glory, which includes all the spiritual and natural wealth available to mankind.

Now that is a different story. I guarantee you it produces awesome results. Jesus said that whatever we ask in His name it would be done. Has anyone ever wondered why that is? What created the visible world? The invisible Word of God did. Basically, the Word of God is the original authority in the earth and the Word has creative powers. Mankind was created to use the creative power of His words. When the Holy Spirit raised Jesus from the dead, God restored all power and authority to the Word of God. When mankind is back in his proper position, using his or her words according to the Word, then the Holy Spirit is free to bring whatever we say to pass. We must be mindful of the things we decide to say.

SEEDS FOR YOUR SOIL

Creative Power of Words: Genesis 1

1. What happens when God says something? How does this relate to mankind?

Matter of Life and Death: Prov. 18:20-21 and Deut. 30:11-20

1. Based on these two passages, how important is the use of words? What implication does that have for anyone that can talk about money?

Understanding the Tongue: James 3

1. How does the Bible describe the tongue?

2. What is the mark of a wise, knowledgeable person?

3. How do we distinguish between God's Wisdom and worldly wisdom?

Recognizing Corrupt Communication: Ephesians 4 and 5

1. The number one result of corrupt communication is confusion. How do we foster peace in our financial lives on a daily basis?

2. What effect should our communication have on us and the people that hear us?

3. List three tools for effective communication as it relates to the money resource.

CHAPTER 6

CHANGING MY APPROACH

How the Proper Attitude and God's Word Can Produce the Right Behavior

Exposè on Conversation

Let's work with the subject of conversation. *Conversation* in our context means conduct or behavior. How many people have read the word *conversation* and automatically associated it with talking? When we research the word in the original Greek translation we find conversation refers to how we act.

> *James 3:13* "Who [is] a wise man and endued with knowledge among you? let him shew out of a good conversation his works with meekness of wisdom."

This verse actually gives a great context clue. It states wisdom and knowledge are demonstrated through a "good conversation." This is not speaking of words. It is speaking of works.

> *Eph. 4:22-24* "...put off concerning the former conversation the old man, which is corrupt according to the

deceitful lusts; And be renewed in the spirit of your mind; And that ye put on the new man, which after God is created in righteousness and true holiness."

Conversation of the Old Man

In layman's terms, this means stop doing what you have been doing. Chances are if you are reading this book then there are some areas of your financial life that are out of order, could be better, or are in shambles. Whatever your situation may be, the solution is to stop doing what you have been doing.

Spirit of Your Mind

Your mind is part natural and part spiritual (Gen. 2:7). The mind is the fiercest battleground of your life. That is why Paul often talks about renewing the mind. That is why the Bible teaches us to meditate on the Word of God. That is why Jesus came to save the souls of men. The soul houses the mind. The thoughts of the mind affect behavior.

Put on the New Man

In layman's terms, this means start dealing with your finances as the Word of God dictates. You cannot continue to manage your money the way you have been managing it and expect different and better results. That is not going to happen.

Righteousness and True Holiness

We change our "conversation" by taking heed to the new spirit man and by not reverting to our old ways and ideas. This new man is exactly like the Adams before they disobeyed God — his or her very nature emanates from God. The new man is clothed in God's righteousness and true holiness. Remember 2 Cor. 5:21 says we have been made the righteousness of God through Jesus Christ.

Ps. 50:23 "Whoso offereth praise glorifieth me: and to him that ordereth [his] conversation [aright] will I shew the salvation of God."

God tells us exactly who will experience salvation — those who get their behavior in order. Salvation is the direct result of proper behavior. First, it is important to understand what exactly salvation is. Salvation is the Hebrew word *yesha* (yeh'-shah), which means liberty, deliverance, prosperity, and safety. It is the Greek word *soteria* (so-tay-ree'-ah), which encompasses deliverance, victory, soundness, preservation, healing, safety, and prosperity.

Have you been delivered from financial bondage — debt? Do you have victory over your countless financial obligations? Are you free from worry when it comes to money matters? Have your finances been preserved by the Almighty God? Do you feel like a whole person when it comes to dealing with the money issue? How safe do you feel about your financial situation? When you think about your personal finances do you think "prosperity"? If you answered no to any of these questions, you need salvation. We might as well stop fooling around. Salvation is about God making you a completely whole man or woman in your spirit, in your mind, and in your finances.

Seeds and Fruit

This chapter is about results so we want to deal with a theme that plays out throughout the Word of God — seeds and fruit. Understanding this concept will help us begin to recognize when we are out of the will of God. We mentioned this concept cursorily, but let's go deeper.

A seed is the specialized part of a plant that produces a new plant. It is made up of an embryo, which has an immature root and stem, a supply of stored food, and a protective covering. How many people know the Word of God is seed? Seeds must be cultivated —

brought from immaturity to perfection — and this is not an overnight process or special "feeling." How many people know the Word of God is spiritual food? It is a supply of stored food. How many people know Jesus died for all the sin of the entire world and by accepting Him as your sacrifice, God has absolutely forgotten your sins because you are covered by the blood of Jesus? His blood is a protective covering.

Fruit is from the Latin word *frui*, which means enjoy. Fruit is intended to be enjoyed or experienced. Now, there are good and bad experiences and fruit is the result of the seed. In fact, the word *result* is defined as fruit. God declares in Isa. 57:19, "I create the fruit (results, consequences) of the lips (words, seed)..." Understand that everything you produce is the fruit or result or consequence of the seed you are using. The Word declares you (not anyone else) will (100 percent of the time) eat the fruit of that which your seed produces!

Absolutely nothing in this earth can live without a seed. Everything you are dealing with at this minute came from a seed. This book, your computer screen, your telephone, your desk, your family all are the result of a seed. Seeds represent a foundation. Seeds are the beginning of life, but they can also result in death. Jesus said in John 6:63, "...the words (seeds) that I speak unto you, they are spirit, and they are life." If we plant bad seeds (i.e., words not according to the Word of God), we reap bad fruit.

How Do I Know If I Am Thinking and Speaking the Right Things?

Are you a child of God? If so, then you need to study to show yourself approved (2 Tim. 2:15) and ask the Spirit to teach you the Word. If you are not a child of God, then you need to accept Jesus Christ and the forgiveness that comes with His package. You must also receive the Spirit of God to illuminate the Word of God in your life.

Without the Spirit's illumination it is tough to know whether what you are thinking and saying lines up with the Word.

Understand this: God has set a universal order in place. Whether you believe Him or not, you cannot change the consequences of your actions. This is why some people can still be very successful (at least in man's eyes) and not know Jesus. This is why some people who claim to know Jesus appear to be very unsuccessful while others are prospering. To know what you are thinking and speaking into your life, you have to examine your own behavior. Matt. 12:33 says, "...for the tree (person) is known by his fruit (results)." Let's go to a popular passage of scripture.

> *Gal. 5:19-21a* "Now the works of the flesh (read: mind and body) are manifest (read: results), which are these;

- adultery — sleeping with someone else's spouse or seriously entertaining the thought of sleeping with someone else's spouse,
- fornication — sleeping with someone outside of marriage or seriously entertaining the thought of sleeping with someone outside of marriage,
- uncleanness — behavior contrary to the Word of God,
- lasciviousness — intense, undisciplined desire; usually sexual, but can apply to anything we uncontrollably want, like things we buy,
- idolatry — putting people, places, things, money, and so forth before God,
- witchcraft — the psychic hotline and the daily horoscope,
- hatred — treating certain types of people better than you treat other types of people,
- variance — dissension, discord, confusion,
- emulations — trying to be like other people instead of being who God created you to be,

- ⚶ wrath — "I'm going to get you back!",
- ⚶ strife — bitter conflict,
- ⚶ seditions — insurrection against lawful authorities,
- ⚶ heresies — doctrine against the gospel of Jesus Christ,
- ⚶ envying — jealousy,
- ⚶ murders — to kill with malice; can include killing the character or spirit of another,
- ⚶ drunkenness — loss of mental and/or physical control; typically through alcohol though one can be "drunk" with pride or other attitudes,
- ⚶ revellings — noisy partying,
- ⚶ and such like — all other things that are contrary to the order God established for mankind.

Gal. 5:21b-23 "...they which do (practice on a regular basis without changing) such things shall not inherit the kingdom of God. But the fruit (result) of the Spirit is

- ⚶ love — treating people like they should be treated; love is not a feeling,
- ⚶ joy — state of happiness (Are you truly happy about your financial situation?),
- ⚶ peace — state of quietness and calm (Are you in a state of confusion about your financial situation?),
- ⚶ longsuffering — patience (Are you patient enough to realize you cannot buy everything at one time?),
- ⚶ gentleness — mild-mannered,
- ⚶ goodness — bountifulness; abundance; prosperity (Does this sound like your financial situation?),
- ⚶ faith — confidence in the Word of God, not your own understanding (Can you stand on God's Word concerning finances?)

- ✷ meekness — not arrogant; teachable in the things of God (Are you willing to learn about finances?),
- ✷ temperance — self-control; ability to follow God's lead and not your own. (Do you buy what you want when you want to regardless of what makes sense in the larger picture?)

> *Gal. 5:24* "...they that are Christ's (the chosen ones; righteous ones; children of God) have crucified the flesh (changed their behavior) with the affections (emotions) and lusts (desires)."

Saints, our thoughts and words lead directly to our behavior. God's Spirit lives in us and He, through that Spirit, wants to teach us how to exemplify His behavior right here in the earth. When we can take an honest look at ourselves and stop blaming other people or our environment, then we will begin to mature in how we approach the money issue. We must personally seek the illumination of the Word of God by the Holy Spirit.

The Essence of Financial Freedom: Obedience

This may be the pivotal point in this book: Complete financial freedom for the Christian begins with obedience to the Word of God. Many of us want God to bless us and bless us and bless us some more, but we have yet to obey Him in the areas of our lives where He has called us to obedience. We are going to see what the Word says about the link between obedience and financial freedom. I call Deuteronomy 28 the modern day Christian's "bless me" chapter. It is comical to me that nobody ever reads the other 80 percent of the chapter that deals with curses. First, let's deal with the "bless me" stanza.

> *Deut. 28:1-2* "And it shall come to pass, if thou shalt hearken diligently unto the voice of the Lord thy God,

to observe [and] to do all his commandments which
I command thee this day, that the Lord thy God will set
thee on high above all nations of the earth: And all these
blessings shall come on thee, and overtake thee, if thou
shalt hearken unto the voice of the Lord thy God."

If is such a small word, but it has great implications. If you have not
noticed anything about God, notice this: everything God declares
has a contingency attached to it. Give and you will receive. Knock
and the door will be opened. Seek and you will find. God works with
if/then statements.

The contingency in this scripture revolves around hearkening
diligently to the voice of the Lord. Sound familiar? This is a command to obey the Word of God. This is a call to action. Only when
obedience is in place does blessing show up. Obedience precedes
blessing.

Deut. 28:3-6 then goes on to talk about all the areas in which an
obedient person would be blessed: in the city, in the suburbs, in the
country, with children, in work, in possessions, with finances, going
in, and coming out. After that, verses 7 through 14 tell us what the
Lord does on behalf of an obedient person: causes their enemies to
fall before them; blesses their investments; blesses all they do; blesses them as they navigate life; establishes them as holy; makes them
plenteous in goods, plenteous in children, and plenty productive;
opens the windows of heaven both naturally and spiritually; makes
them a lender not a borrower; and establishes them as the standard
of excellence. In other words, an obedient person becomes completely financially free.

To contrast, we need to examine verses 15 through 68. The first
thing to notice is the passage begins with the word *but*. My pastor
likes to say, "When you see *but*, you can basically cancel everything
that was said before it." The *but* in this case refers to anyone — Chris-

tian or otherwise — who does not abide by the Word of God. In verses 15 through 26, God completely cancels all the good stuff we just mentioned. But God does not stop there. He spends a whopping 80 percent of the chapter outlining the curses that come along with being disobedient. What we see is that He added quite a few items: sickness, insanity, blindness, fear, oppression, poverty, unfaithfulness, weariness, embarrassment, unproductiveness, want, lack, indebtedness, disunity, and destruction. In other words, disobedience leads to complete financial dysfunction and bondage.

Behavioral Fundamentals:
The Ant, The Conies, The Locusts, and The Spider

Prov. 30:24-28 "There be four [things which are] little upon the earth, but they [are] exceeding wise: The ants [are] a people not strong, yet they prepare their meat in the summer; The conies [are but] a feeble folk, yet make they their houses in the rocks; The locusts have no king, yet go they forth all of them by bands; The spider taketh hold with her hands, and is in kings' palaces."

Our animal and insect friends exhibit the four fundamental P's to financial success — preparation (ant), prudence (conies), partnership (locusts), and productivity (spider). We will deal with each one in turn.

Ants

Our ant friend anticipates winter's harshness or, better said, realizes that summer does not last all year. Being the exceedingly wise creature she is, she prepares her resources in the summer so she does not lack resources in the winter. Another interesting note about ant behavior is that ants can find the shortest path from a food source to the nest without using visual cues. Also, they can adapt to changes in the environment. For example, they will find a new shortest path if the old one becomes blocked.[F]

Conies

The conies, otherwise known as rock badgers, exercise prudence. They recognize the state of their resources and make a good judgment as to how to effectively use those resources. Crags and crevices of rocky outcrops and cliffs are ideal for the rock badger because he is a slow-moving, natural target for predators. The inhospitable environment ensures that enemies keep their distance. The home of the rock badger also provides ideal protection from wind and rain. For these reasons the badger spends most of his time in his rocky home. The only time he ventures forth is when he goes out looking for food.[G]

Locusts

The locusts act in unity. They value the concept of partnership. Now they aren't necessarily the farmer's best friends, but they work the partnership principle to a tee. Locusts can inflict widespread and severe damage to pastures, cereal crops, and forage crops. In closely settled areas they may also cause considerable damage to vegetable and orchard crops. When locust population density is high they form into gregariously behaving bands of nymphs or swarms of adults. Dense aggregations of locust nymphs (hoppers) are called bands. Damage by bands is usually confined to pasture, although crops, particularly young winter cereals, are susceptible. Bands may extend over several miles and are often visible from the air. Alternatively, an aggregation of adult locusts is called a swarm. A swarm may consist of millions of locusts and can cover an area of several square miles. A large swarm of adult locusts can consume several tons of plant material every day, quickly devastating any crops or pastures in their path.[H]

Spiders

The spider is all about productivity. She works with her hands. Hard work doing exactly what she was created to do resulted in fellowship with royalty. Spiders produce silk, which is secreted as a liquid through the spinnerets and hardens on contact with air. Different spiders produce different types and textures of silk, which may be used to construct snares or webs, egg sacs, draglines, and ballooning threads. Some spiders use web snares to trap prey and all construct a silk sac to deposit eggs. Many spiders attach draglines of silk to the substrate at intervals wherever they go, appearing to have a silk thread to hang onto when knocked from their perch. Some spiderlings sail through the air (ballooning) on wind currents. Young spiders climb to a high point and release silk strands until the drag from the wind is sufficient to support their weight. Then, they release their hold and sail away, often for considerable distances. These ballooning threads (gossamer) can fill the air on clear days as spiderlings disperse to new areas.[1]

Through these simple examples, the Holy Spirit has given us the blueprint for establishing a strong financial foundation and operating in the prosperous environment God intended for us.

Stop Digging!

SEEDS FOR YOUR SOIL

Conversation (Behavior): Philippians 3

1. What types of people should we beware of as believers? How does that enhance our ability to behave properly?

2. Verse 20 suggests that our behavior should reflect heaven. How do we facilitate that?

Fostering Good Conversation: Galatians 5 and 6

1. Gal. 5:1 suggests that even after being made debt free, one can still end up back in debt. How does one break the chains of digger behavior once and for all?

2. What type of planting actions result in everlasting life?

Obedience, the First and Only Commandment: Eccl. 12:13-14, John 14:6-21, and 1 John 2 and 3

1. Eccl. 12:13-14 sum up the whole duty of man. John 14:6-21 reinforces the thought. 1 John 2 and 3 bring us home. How do these passages relate to the believer's ability to truly experience abundance and financial freedom?

104

PART III

GETTING MY SOIL READY

The Four P's to Reestablishing a Strong Financial Foundation

CHAPTER 7

NO PLAN,
NO PROGRESS

Why God Wants Me to Start Where I Am

Plan!

How many people are floating through life without a plan? What do you want to be when you grow up? Where will you be five years from now? Ten? Thirty? What is the vision for your life? How much money do you need to make it happen? Do you know the answer to these questions? In my experience many individuals do not.

One of the first questions I ask people when I counsel them on their finances is, "What are you trying to do?" The troubled expression that usually greets me says, "You know, Cliff, I've never really thought about that!" Many people are looking for God to drop some money out of the sky, yet they have no purpose for the money besides the plan to buy some more stuff. Many of our prayers sound a lot like this: "God, I really *need* some money to pay these bills. Please send some money my way. Let the money blessings fall down from the sky!"

Let's note two things. First, there is no money in the sky. The earth is money. Second, many of us are not prepared to handle money so explain to me again why it is a *need*! Now, you are probably thinking, "I *need* to pay my bills!" But God believes it is unwise to lack an appropriate plan. In fact, in Isaiah we find that God declares the end from the beginning (Isa. 46:10). In other words, God is a planner. Remember that idea about being made in His image and after His likeness?

When Preparation Meets Opportunity

When preparation meets opportunity, success is right around the corner. What is the first thing wise people do? Prepare! As we make decisions to grow — mentally, physically, spiritually, or financially — we must properly plan. Here are some personal examples.

- Mentally — When I decided to attend graduate school, I had to prepare my mind and my finances. I had to prepare to adjust to the life of a student again.
- Physically — When I get ready to step out on the basketball court, I have to prepare my body with stretching so I do not pull any muscles.
- Spiritually — When I made a decision to truly build a relationship with my Father, I had to prepare my heart and mind to receive instruction that is sometimes contrary to what I feel like doing.
- Financially — To get to multimillionaire status, I have adequately prepared my budget and investment plan as well as my plans to generate multiple sources of income. Becoming debt-free and reaching multimillionaire status does not just happen. It begins with a plan.

Preparation in Action

If we went through every story in the Bible, we would see God is all about preparation and having a plan. Let's look again at the events of Genesis 1 and Genesis 2:1-3. In the entire account of what most call "The Creation" (what I call the reestablishment of order in the earth), we witness an example of God's focus on preparation. Each "evening and morning" builds on that which was prepared on the prior "evening and morning."

Let us take a closer look at the "week."

- Day 1: Appearance of Light (Wisdom or Word of God) and the separation of "Light" from the spiritual darkness ushered in by Satan when he fell from heaven (Luke 10:18).
- Day 2: Making of firmament (arch of the sky; Heaven) and the dividing of the waters above and below the firmament.
- Day 3: Gathering of the waters (seas) below the firmament, the appearance of dry land (earth), then grass, herb yielding seed, and fruit trees able to grow exponentially, each after its own kind.
- Day 4: Lights in the firmament (sun, moon, and stars) for signs, seasons, days, and years and to give natural light to the earth.
- Day 5: The creatures of the seas and the winged fowl of the skies both brought forth in abundance by the water.
- Day 6: Living creatures, cattle, and creeping things brought forth by the earth. Mankind in spirit, made in God's image and after God's likeness, created by God, made by His Word and given dominion over everything created before him.
- Day 7: God enters into rest because he has given his greatest creation complete control and stewardship over all the things He created on Days 1 through 6.

That was a magnificent display so we want to make sure we saw what we needed to see in that sequence.

The Concept of Preparation

First, God needed the true Light to restore order in the earth, which was in a state of chaos. Second, He needed to shape the earth, which was "without form." Third, he had to separate the water from the dry land in order for it to bring forth vegetation. Fourth, once vegetation was present it needed natural light to grow. Fifth, now that there was natural light, the creatures of both the sea and sky could come forth. Sixth, now that vegetation was sprouting, the creatures of the earth could come forth. Additionally, God's spiritual sons could be created because all of the things they would be created to take care of were adequately prepared and in place. Lastly, God rested because He gave everything to us. In a way, we are His protégès.

Law of Increase

Everything God made is based on the concept of investment, multiplication, exponential growth, and things reproducing after their own kind. Seeds represent an investment. Seeds have even more seeds in them and those seeds have even more seeds in them. Let me break it down like this. I begin with 1 apple seed. That seed grows into a tree with 50 apples. There are 5 seeds in each apple. I now have 250 apple seeds. I plant those 250 seeds. Now I have an orchard and another 62,500 apple seeds. I plant those seeds and receive 15,625,000 apple seeds, not to mention the fruit I am enjoying...Need we go any further?

God did not create us to dig — over consume. He created us to plant — invest in people, in ourselves, with our money, and so forth. You see, we are free to enjoy the fruit, but we must stop eating the seeds. If you are spending all your money or spending money you do not have, then you are eating the seeds. According to God's system, we must first give or invest. Again, seeds produce after their own kind (i.e., money makes money just like apple seeds make apples, not oranges). There must be a period of preparation.

In Case You Thought I Was Kidding about Preparation

Exod. 23:20-22 "Behold, I send an Angel before thee,
to keep thee in the way, and to bring thee into the place

which I have prepared. Beware (be aware) of him, and obey his voice, provoke him not; for he will not pardon your transgressions: for my name [is] in him. But if thou shalt indeed obey his voice and do all that I speak; then I will be an enemy unto thine enemies, and an adversary unto thine adversaries."

God is talking to Moses here, but really He is talking to us as believers. In this passage, He is referring to the Promised Land. Notice He had prepared the land. How many people know the Promised Land had people already living there? Moreover, these people were mighty men and women who had built great, intimidating cities and had riches to no end. Prov. 13:22b says, "The wealth of the sinner [is] laid up (prepared) for the just (sons of God, saints)." God has already prepared a place of abundance and exponential growth for us. Are we willing to obey His voice?

Notice how God sent an angel before Moses. Ps. 91:11-12 reads, "For he shall give his angels charge over thee, to keep thee in all thy ways. They shall bear thee up in [their] hands, lest thou dash thy foot against a stone." Hebrews 1:14 reads, "Are they (the angels) not all ministering (serving) spirits, sent forth to minister for them who shall be heirs of salvation?" How many people know you have supernatural guardians that move according to your words? When we speak the Word of God, our angels are moving on our behalf. When we speak against the Word of God, we give the devil's crew of angels permission to work. Angels were created to make sure we get where God intends for us to go safe and sound. However, we must speak and perform according to the Word of God to be protected. Sound familiar? Again, the destination is already prepared.

Another "P" Word
Jesus had a way of preparing himself for His work. Want to guess

what His method was? Yes. It is definitely another "P" word. For all my rocket scientists, the word is *prayer*. Let's get a better understanding of the basics of prayer.

Prayer is two-way communication between man and God. Prayer involves both talking and listening. This is an important point: we pray so we can hear from God. Prayer is not designed for us to loft up miscellaneous requests and hope something good happens. Many times God's response to our prayers is to tell us to stop praying and get up to do something. Many times there is no response. God is saying, "You already know what you need to do. Why are you still talking to me?" As it relates to our finances, God is simply telling us to make a plan. Stop praying about the things you can control. Prepare a plan and work it.

Prayer is what allows God to legally move in the earth. Remember what we learned about our words? As a born again believer, you literally pray — communicate with God — every time you open your mouth. That should certainly make us watch what we say. Not only that, but you are in prayer every time you are in a position to hear from God, which should be always. Right? Again, man is the steward/caretaker of the earth and must grant the Holy Spirit permission to move in the natural realm. All spirits need permission to operate in the natural realm and they receive permission through our words. That, of course, begs the question: If God is the Creator of all things visible and invisible, why does He need permission to do stuff in the earth? He should be able to do whatever He wants to do! One thing God has never done is violate His Word. In the book of Genesis, God gave mankind dominion over all the wealth in the earth. This is man's show. If God operates in the earth outside of the order He established when He spoke, then He would be acting against His Word!

We must embrace the reality we were actually created to commune with God. We were created to pray. It was part of the design.

We should understand it is impossible to succeed without prayer. Let us answer an age-old question: Where does God dwell? Eph. 2:21-22 says, "...all the building (all believers) fitly framed together groweth unto an holy temple in the Lord...ye are also builded together for an habitation of God through the Spirit." 1 Cor. 3:16-17 says, "Know ye not that ye are the temple of God, and that the Spirit of God dwelleth in you? If any man defile the temple of God, him shall God destroy; for the temple of God is holy, which temple ye are."

God intricately designed mankind so He himself could actually live in mankind through His Spirit. God dwells in born again believers through the Holy Spirit. We, as a called out people, make up the house of God, not the physical "church" building. Well, what does He say concerning His house? In Matt. 21:13, Jesus references a verse in Isaiah (56:7) that describes God's house. "Even them will I bring to my holy mountain, and make them joyful in my house of prayer: their burnt offerings and their sacrifices [shall be] accepted upon mine altar; for mine house shall be called an house of prayer for all people."

The house of prayer is actually not the building. We and all other believers make up the house of prayer. We are the place where mankind can commune with God. We were, in fact, created to communicate with God. What broke the communication was a lack of holiness. The holiness problem was rectified through Christ.

Because we were created to pray we must always pray.

2 Thess. 5:17: "Pray without ceasing."

Luke 18:1b: "Men ought always to pray, and not to faint."

Luke 21:36a: "Watch ye therefore, and pray always."

Rom. 12:12b: "Continuing instant in prayer."

Acts 6:4a: "But we will give ourselves continually in prayer."

Eph. 6:18a: "Praying always with all prayer and supplication in the Spirit."

Remember, prayer is a two-way communication. As long as you are in position to hear from God, you are in prayer.

Finally, we should know the purpose of prayer. We don't need prayer and faith for things we can attain with our God-given natural ability. Some things we just need to do. Pray for those things that are beyond your natural ability and those things you cannot control. Pray for other people; pray against the works of the enemy; pray for revelation knowledge of the Word of God; pray for natural ideas and spiritual insight. Give the Spirit of God something to do. He likes to work! Instead of complaining about your financial situation, pray about it. Once you get the solution, go to work. God is not going to plan it out for you. However, He will indeed give you favor and insights as you plan it out.

The Quiet Time of Prayer
Matt. 6:6-8 "But thou, when thou prayest, enter into thy closet, and when thou hast shut thy door, pray to thy Father which is in secret; and thy Father which seeth in secret shall reward thee openly. But when ye pray, use not vain repetitions, as the heathen do: for they think they shall be heard for their much speaking. Be not ye therefore like unto them: for your Father knoweth what things ye have need of, before ye ask him."

When Thou Prayest
This is referring specifically to our daily prayer life. (There are times

for public prayer.) This is our intimate time with God when we can share personal business. God wants to hear what is on our hearts (not vain repetitions) in secret. Jesus always went away from the masses for personal prayer. God desires a close one-to-one relationship with us. We learn to acknowledge God through our relationship with Him.

Open Rewards

As we continue to seek God in prayer, He says He will reward us openly! The things we believe Him for through prayer in faith will manifest themselves in the natural realm and others will see it. If we desire a breakthrough in how we approach money, this is an effective method to get us started. God will begin to show you the areas where you need help. He will begin to put people in your life that have the expertise you need. He will teach you the importance of financial planning and preparation for the future. These are the "open rewards." People will see the changes you have made and will be amazed. They will want to know how you did it. They might offer to pay you to help them get where you are!

Open Your Mouth

God knows what we need, but He will do nothing unless we ask. Now we see the reference to "vain repetitions" and "much speaking." We also see the word "ask." All of these things suggest we must speak to God out loud (not that there are not times for silent prayer). Remember God's order of operation — He thinks, then speaks, then the Spirit moves. Get used to talking to God out loud. Words are spiritual and unleash power in the earth. Words represent dominion.

Preparation and Resources

The Word of God consistently establishes the link between preparation and resources. Many scriptures, such as the "lay not up treasures on earth" verse we already discussed, have been completely taken out of context. It is almost a ridiculous notion not to recognize the importance of preparing and planning out the use of resources. Biblical examples abound.

> *Prov. 13:22* "A good [man] leaveth an inheritance to his children's children..."

Inheritance

I was thinking about all the great things we can siphon out of this verse. But I kept coming back to this: How can somebody leave an inheritance for their grandchildren if they do not prepare for the future by storing up resources and investing?

> *Prov. 24:27* "Prepare thy work without, and make it fit for thyself in the field; and afterwards build thine house."

Afterwards

A lot of people have a problem with this word. This is a "right now" society. I want what I want right now! We rarely have a sense for the long-term effects of our actions. As Pastor Chuck of the Gary Christian Center put it, we continue to make short-term decisions that have dire long-term effects.

> *Luke 14:28* "For which of you, intending to build a tower, sitteth not down first, and counteth the cost, whether he have [sufficient] to finish [it]?"

Count the Cost

Jesus is asking a rhetorical question, yet it is a question we should all consider. We have built plenty of towers without counting the cost.

We owe money on the car. We owe money on the house. We owe money on the very clothes we are wearing. We owe money on the vacation we took two years ago. We do not plan. We just purchase.

> *John 14:2-4* "In my Father's house are many mansions: if [it were] not [so], I would have told you. I go to prepare a place for you. And if I go and prepare a place for you, I will come again, and receive you unto myself; that where I am, [there] ye may be also. And whither I go ye know, and the way ye know."

Jesus is Preparing Right Now

This is deep to me. I used to wonder about this place Jesus said He was going off to prepare. A lot of my confusion had to do with this when-I-get-to-heaven doctrine that pervades many church assemblies. A closer read of the Bible will reveals that God created mankind to inhabit the earth, not heaven. Heaven is not man's destination. The earth is man's inheritance and destiny. In Rev. *21:1-5*, we find John describing a new heaven and a new earth. He also saw the holy city of God descending from heaven to earth and this is where God dwells with His people forever. So what is Jesus doing with His resources? He is preparing, as all wise people do, for the future.

SEEDS FOR YOUR SOIL

God Prepares: Isa. 46:3-13 and Genesis 1

1. God starts with an end or goal in mind and plans according
   to the goal. In Isaiah 46, the goal is salvation for Israel.
   Everything until that takes place is a means to an end. In
   Genesis 1, the goal is to furnish mankind with the ability to
   experience the abundance and creativity of God. Everything
   up until God spoke mankind into existence was just a
   means to an end. How can we apply that lesson to our lives?

The Role of Prayer in Preparation: Matt. 6:6 - 8

1. Take this time to pray to God for guidance concerning how
   you should plan your finances for the present as well as the
   future.

CHAPTER 8

A Steward Must Exercise Wisdoom

God's Attitude Toward Prudence

What Is Prudence?

Prudence is skill and good judgment in the use of resources. It is also caution or circumspection regarding danger or risk. Remember the rock badgers? They recognize they are feeble. However, they have enough sense to use the resources God gave them to build solid protection that will guard them from the inherent dangers and risks of life. Do we exercise that much good sense in our lives? How well are we using the resources we have? These are compelling questions. Why? Because when we misuse the resources God already gave us, God is not obligated to give us more. (Minister Shundrawn addresses this in *Start Planting!*) Prudence is all about anticipation and foresight. We can relate it to the action verb *predict*. *Predict* means to declare in advance; to foretell (to tell beforehand; to prophesy); and to exercise foresight.

The Word of God is prophetic; it is declared in advance. How many people know God tells us the ending from the beginning? He always says "if" you do this, "then" this will happen. "If" you do that, "then" the result will be different. God does not move in mysterious ways. He tells us point blank how certain behavior leads to certain results. Therefore, our ability to anticipate and be prudent is tied up in our faith or confidence in the Word of God. The Word of God holds the key to everything that is considered good judgment. It explains how to properly use the resources God gave us. The Word of God is Wisdom!

Five Elements of Prudence

The book of Proverbs, which many people call the book of wisdom (I say the whole Book is wisdom), outlines some of the characteristics of a prudent person. A closer examination reveals a prudent person receives instruction, owns knowledge, utilizes knowledge, does not believe everything he or she hears, and is forward looking.

> *Prov. 15:5* "A fool despiseth his father's instruction: but he that regardeth (takes heed to) reproof (correction) is prudent."

Receives Instruction

A prudent person is ready to receive instruction and correction. How many people know you do not need instructions when you are already operating correctly? If you are my child and I have already taught you how to wash the dishes, the only other time I will give you instructions about the dishes is if I find my favorite bowl with a bunch of gunk in it! You are obviously doing something wrong and you must be corrected. If you are struggling to pay your monthly bills, worried about your financial future, or do not have a grip on your debt (spending), you need some instructions. Most of all you need to follow the instructions.

> *Prov. 18:15* "The heart of the prudent getteth knowledge; and the ear of the wise seeketh knowledge."

Owns Knowledge

The word *heart* is the Hebrew word *leb* (labe), which refers to the will, intellect, and emotions of a person. That word *getteth* is the Hebrew word *qanah* (kaw-naw'), which literally means to possess or own. Ownership implies a purchase. Are we applying our heart to knowledge? What are we purchasing to further our financial acuity? Are we investing in knowledge of personal finances? Do we think we can somehow just figure it out? Are our will, intellect, and emotions focused on laying a financial foundation or are we content to keep doing what we have been doing?

> *Prov. 13:16* "Every prudent [man] dealeth with knowledge: but a fool layeth open [his] folly (lack of good sense and foresight)."

Utilizes Knowledge

The mark of operating prudently is "dealing with knowledge," which simply means our words and actions reflect the things we know to be true. It manifests in the ability to anticipate situations and circumstances. In chapter 2, we learned God's people are useless because they lack knowledge and the reason they lack knowledge is because they reject the knowledge that is available to them (Hos. 4:6). This book is meant provide a foundation of financial knowledge, but the sign of a prudent person will reveal itself in a person's willingness to use the knowledge and, more importantly, build on it.

> *Prov. 14:15* "The simple believeth every word: but the prudent [man] looketh well (attentively) to his going."

Does Not Believe Everything He or She Hears

The prudent person confirms the things others speak with the Word of God. He or she is attentive to that which God says about the matter. This is an absolutely crucial cog in our quest to walk in financial freedom. Adopting God's attitude toward money challenges a vast majority of our country's population. They don't understand money. They don't know what to say about money. They cannot decipher the truth about money so they say things like, "I will always be broke!" 1 John 4:1a reads, "Beloved, believe not every spirit, but try (read: examine them against the Word of God) the spirits whether they are of God." How many people know words are spirits (John 6:63 and 2 Thess. 2:8)? Again, our words release activity in the spirit realm. Words have results already tied to them, which were ordained by God (Isa. 57:19). When our words are not God's words, we will not and should not expect to receive God's things. Good judgment and foresight comes directly from the Word of God. All words that are not in agreement with the Word result in folly.

> *Prov. 22:3* "A prudent [man] foreseeth (predicts) the evil, and hideth himself: but the simple pass on, and are punished."

Forward Looking

When we decide to exercise good judgment and circumspection (meditating on the Word of God), we can clearly see "the evil" and choose to avoid it. God has endowed us with His very own Spirit, which gives us superior insight into any and all elements of this earthly existence. This includes money. In Heb. 5:12-14 and 6:1-3, Paul is warning the church folks about getting stuck in elementary aspects of the life of Christianity, such as abundance. In this brief passage, he states something I have always thought was profound and now think is relevant to Prov. 22:3. Paul says those who are ready to receive the real "meat" of the gospel of Christ are people "who by reason of use have their senses exercised to discern both good and evil." Some of us continue to make questionable financial decisions because we have not exercised the wise advice given to us by experts in the field. Some of us continue to make problematic financial commitments because we do not use the Word of God as a basis for the choices we make. We have no vision beyond that which we can physically see. Does that sound familiar? How can we look forward when we cannot see past the here and now?

Prudence on Display: Joshua

There are numerous examples in the Bible of people who displayed prudence. We want to look at the life of Joshua. Joshua was an awesome man of God. In fact, Joshua was a type, or a foreshadowing, of Jesus. When we research the meanings of the names *Joshua* and *Jesus* we find they both mean "God is salvation." Joshua was charged with the job of leading the children of Israel into the land God promised them — God's salvation. In comparison, Jesus is now the way that leads to God's salvation. More importantly, this is now the Joshua Age, if you will, because the ministry of Jesus (God's salvation) belongs squarely to those that have been elected into God's church. Furthermore, Joshua understood that true leadership was about service. We only need to look at Jesus to know that God's definition of leadership is tied up in the concept of service.

Receiving Instruction

We read about Joshua for the first time in Exodus 17. God had triumphantly delivered the children of Israel from the hands of the Egyptians. As the people of God lodged in Rephidim, the Amalekites came in to fight them. It is unclear what the motives of the Amalekites were. What is clear is it was time to go to war. [Just a preparation aside: The children of Israel came out of Egypt armed for battle (Exod. 13:18). God does not leave His people unprepared!] Well, what was Joshua's role in the war? He was actually the leader of the mission. He received his instructions from Moses and verse

10 declares that he "did as Moses said to him." In other words, just because he was the leader did not mean that he could do whatever he wanted to do because he had dominion in the earth. Joshua was under authority and only under that authority was he successful.

The next time we find Joshua we learn a little more about his relationship to Moses. We discover Joshua is Moses' minister. That word *minister* is the Hebrew word *sharath* (shaw-rath'), which means server or waiter. So while being a minister is a role of leadership, it is ultimately about being a server. Being a server means being attentive to the needs of others. Now between the time of the battle and this revelation about Joshua, God reunited Moses with his family, spoke the ten commandments to the congregation of Israel from Mt. Sinai, and delivered the rest of the law to Moses (because the people could not bear to hear anymore). God then called Moses up into Mt. Sinai for some one-on-one time. Before he went, Moses spoke the law of God to the people, wrote down the law of God, and sealed the covenant with the blood of a sacrifice. The scripture says that when Moses rose up to go into the mountain, Joshua rose up with him. Why? To be in a position to receive instructions. Moses spent forty days and forty nights in the presence of the Lord receiving instructions on how to construct the tabernacle of the Lord. Joshua spent that time patiently waiting, constantly in position to receive the next set of instructions from Moses.

Owning Knowledge

Moving right along, Joshua really shows us something the next time we see him. Moses and Joshua return to the people after spending such a long time at Mt. Sinai. The people had apparently grown tired of waiting and decided to make their own god out of a golden calf. (That is a word for someone. Many of us create "gods" because we do not have the patience to wait on what God is doing on our behalf.) Because of this rebellion, God plagued the people, but, more importantly, removed his tabernacle from the midst of the people. The tabernacle represented the very presence of God. With the tabernacle now outside of the camp, Moses went out to meet with God. Guess who was with him. That's correct: Joshua. Exod. 33:11 reads, "And the Lord spake unto Moses face to face, as a man speaketh unto his friend. And he (Moses) turned again into the camp: but his servant Joshua, the son of Nun, a young man, departed not out of the tabernacle." There is a lot to this verse, but let's concentrate on the phrase "departed not out of the tabernacle." We can read that as saying, "departed not out of the presence of the Lord." I believe Joshua recognized something all believers must recognize to be successful in this life: owning or possessing the knowledge of God begins in the very presence of God.

Using Knowledge

Proper use of knowledge confirms possession. In Numbers 11, after God had continually put up with the grumbling of the children of Israel, we find Moses growing weary of the complaints and asking God to kill him so he does not have to deal with it anymore. God then told Moses to gather seventy elders of the people to the tabernacle and promised to place His Spirit upon them to relieve Moses. When the elders were gathered, the Lord descended in a cloud and made His Spirit rest upon the elders and immediately they began to declare the truth of God. There were actually only sixty-eight elders at the meeting. Eldad and Medad remained in the camp. However, God was not limited to the "church building" so we learn that Eldad and Medad were declaring the truth of God in the camp because the Spirit rested upon them too. (They were, after all, part of the seventy!) A young man came running out to Moses to tell him Eldad and Medad were prophesying in the camp. This is where we see Joshua had not quite possessed the knowledge of God yet. Numbers 11:28 reads, "And Joshua the son of Nun, the servant of Moses,

[one] of his young men, answered and said, My lord Moses, forbid them." Joshua had limited the move of God to the "church building." He did not realize God is not a God of limitations. He did not realize that God is able to do exceedingly above all we ask or think. Joshua did not properly use knowledge. If you read the actual book of Joshua, you will see Joshua eventually figured out how to use knowledge properly.

Not Believing Everything You Hear

Shortly after this episode, we see God is preparing to take the children of Israel into the Promised Land. In preparation, God instructed Moses to send twelve spies, one from each tribe, to search out the land of Canaan. Joshua was among the twelve spies. The Bible declares that after forty days they returned from their journey. Now mind you, God had repeatedly told the children of Israel He would "drive out the inhabitants of the land" and not to worry about anything. The spies returned with a report that confirmed the contents of the land. However, they added a word — nevertheless — and omitted God's Word concerning the situation. In Numbers 13:28a the spies say, "Nevertheless the people [be] strong that dwell in the land, and the cities [are] walled, [and] very great." This negativity stirred up fear in the congregation. In the midst of this, Caleb pronouncd, "Let us go up at once, and possess it; for we are well able to overcome it." However, the ten dissenters had the ears of the people and caused them to cry all night due to the "impossible" situation that stood before them. Joshua and Caleb began to declare the Word of the Lord concerning Israel's plight. They continued to confirm the goodness of the land and the fact that the Lord was with them so there was no reason to fear. Alas, the people sought to stone Joshua and Caleb with stones. God had seen enough. He testified that no one twenty years of age and older would enter in to the land of promise, but they would all die in the wilderness because they had not believed what God had told them. Everyone was subject to this declaration except Joshua and Caleb.

Looking Ahead

Now after this declaration by God, the people mourned. Nevertheless, the Word had gone forth and God's will would be accomplished. Their refusal to rely on God destroyed their lives, but the children of Israel continued to disrespect God. Twelve chapters later, by the end of chapter 26, 40 years had passed and all of those people that were twenty years old and over at the time of God's proclamation had died in the wilderness except for Caleb and Joshua. Finally, in Numb. 27:16-17, Moses proclaims to God, "Let the Lord, the God of the spirits of all flesh, set a man over the congregation, Which may go out before them, and which may go in before them, and which may lead them out, and which may bring them in; that the congregation of the Lord be not as sheep which have no shepherd." Then we see the Lord replies in verses 18 and 19, "Take thee Joshua the son of Nun, a man in whom [is] the spirit, and lay thine hand upon him; And set him before Eleazar the priest, and before all the congregation; and give him a charge in their sight." Well, what was that charge? Joshua would actually be the one to lead the children of Israel into the Promised Land in Moses' stead (Deut. 3:28). After receiving the charge, Joshua still had to be a man of patience and vision. He had to have patience because Moses had to spend some time teaching the new generation of Israelites the statutes of God. Joshua was the new leader, but his authority did not begin until Moses died. He had to have vision because the only thing God told him in Deut. 31:23 was "Be strong and of a good courage: for thou shalt bring the children of Israel into the land which I sware unto them: and I will be with thee." That was it. There was no elaborate blueprint. Why was he able to be a forward-looking man? Deut. 34:9 asserts Joshua was full of the spirit of wisdom. Isn't that what this chapter is all about?

Handling Money with Prudence

Let's review the five elements of prudence: receive instruction; own knowledge; utilize knowledge; do not believe everything you hear; and be forward looking.

Receiving Instruction

Many of us, even with the shaky or less than ideal state of our finances, fundamentally do not believe we need any instruction concerning the money resource. We will never be financially free until we realize we unquestionably do need instruction. But beyond that, we have to be willing to actually follow instructions. A lot of times, our inclination for control and domination will not allow us to humbly receive instruction concerning our money. If we cannot figure it out, we feel like a failure. We are missing the explicit plan of our Father. He did not create us to figure out everything ourselves. He gifted each person with his or her own areas of expertise (we tackle that in the next chapter).

Owning Knowledge

What does it mean to possess something? One definition in *Merriam Webster's Collegiate Dictionary* says to enter into and control firmly. We spent the entire second chapter of this book getting to know money and getting to know God's attitude toward money. But, if we really want to own that knowledge, we must do it in the presence of the Lord. If I do not spend any time in your presence, I will never get to know your attitudes, ideas, and dreams. To grasp God's viewpoint toward money, you must spend time in His presence. See, Joshua was on to something. He realized that to really relate to God he had to spend some time with Him. There is no room for guesswork. This ties in to chapter 4's discussion about the importance of meditating on the Word of God.

Utilizing Knowledge

The principles outlined in this book are unfailing spiritual tools for success. They represent knowledge. But knowledge is abstract unless it is being used. As a matter of fact, knowledge is just information when it is not being used. There is no advantage to having information that is not being used. So we can be informed we should seek God first and establish order in our financial life through changing our overall approach to money, eliminating debt, and crafting a wealth-building plan, but until the wheels are in motion there is no change. Therefore, there is no success.

Do Not Believe Everything You Hear

Plenty of people have an assortment of schemes for wealth building, getting rich quick, canceling debt, and so forth. The key question to ask when entertaining advice concerning how to use your money resource is: Does this agree with God's outlook on money? That is the test. If it does and it is applicable to your situation, implementation will certainly lead to success.

Be Forward Looking

If there are two destructive attitudes that permeate our society, they are instant gratification and selfishness. Everything must be done right now or five minutes ago. Everything is done in a rush. Everything is about my life and how I feel! God does not operate like that. He makes everything beautiful in His time (Eccl. 3:11). Just as Joshua had to be patient and forward looking, we must learn to embrace that reality in our own lives.

The Anti-Prudence: Foolishness

As we read the Bible many of us skip over the word *foolish* like we do the words *wicked* and *unrighteous*. Like me, you may say, "This part is not talking about me!" Boy, have I got news for you. The Bible was written to the people of God. Therefore, if the Holy Spirit has indeed baptized you into the body of Christ, the word *foolish* absolutely has some type of implication for you! A foolish person despises instructions, openly displays a lack of good judgment and foresight, and tends to believe everything he or she hears. Can we see how foolishness is the opposite of prudence?

Despises Instructions

Prov. 15:5 says, "A fool despiseth his father's instruction: but he that regardeth (takes heed to) reproof (correction) is prudent." The word *despises* means to scorn or to reject as unworthy. If someone offers you the correct way to do something and you still do not perform the task correctly, you have despised instructions. A person with financial issues will typically not listen to sound advice. However, if you are eager to improve your financial foundation and grow your wealth, you will be willing to learn.

Lack of Foresight

People who exhibit a lack of foresight live for the moment. The say things like, "You never know how long you'll be here so you might as well enjoy yourself now!" Or, "I want what I want when I want it!" Attitudes like this scream out-sight. These statements represent a complete lack of vision. Everyone who's serious about building wealth has vision!

Easily Persuaded

Some of us move from one get-rich-quick scheme to another. Others of us are completely swayed by the opinions of other people. If we want to experience financial freedom, our persuasion must come from the Holy Spirit. Wealthy people exude confidence in what they know.

Let's summarize. Prudence is skill and good judgment in the use of resources. The underlying principles of prudence manifest in five ways: receiving instruction, possessing knowledge, using knowledge, not being easily persuaded, and being forward looking. This makes the prudence test easy. It begins with being willing to learn something. By learning something, we begin to possess knowledge. When we possess knowledge, we then have the option to use knowledge. When we use knowledge, we are not so quickly convinced by every money scheme that comes along. When we can stay focused, we begin to embrace the bigger picture and look forward. That is prudence!

SEEDS FOR YOUR SOIL

Elements of Prudence:
Prov. 15:5, Prov. 18:15, Prov. 13:16, Prov. 14:15, and Prov. 22:3

1. Assess whether or not you exhibit the elements of prudence in your approach to the money resource. Identify areas of weakness. Pray about them. Craft a strategy to address and strengthen those areas of trouble.

The Prudent Man, Joshua: Exodus, Numbers, and Joshua

1. Really study how Joshua handled himself, the people of God, and his relationship with the Lord. What can we learn from his approach to life that we can apply to our approach to finances?

CHAPTER 9

I'm Not
an Island

How God Feels about Partnership

Island Livin'

Many people believe that if you want something done right, you might as well do it yourself and they operate accordingly. This is entirely anti-biblical. God designed mankind so that we each play a crucial part in the success of everyone else. Specialization asserts that all people are better off if each person specializes in what they are the best at.

Everyday we find out just how uninformed we really are. There is so much we just do not know. Furthermore, it is virtually impossible, or at the very least unreasonable, to think we can learn everything we need to know about all of life's various situations. Nevertheless, *somebody* knows what we do not know. So really all we need to do is hook up with experts in the field — people that specialize — and trust in what they know. For example, imagine my wife and I have just purchased our first home. We have lived in apartments all of our lives so we have no working knowledge of how to manage and maintain a house. If the hot water was off in the apartment, we merely called the landlord and he or she handled everything. The cost to us was the price of a local phone call (and rent of course). Now, our hot water is off and we have no idea how a hot water heater works. What do we do? We get out there and find a specialist in hot water heaters. Of course, we could do some research and try to figure out what to do. However, I believe our time would be best spent by continuing to get paid to specialize in what we are the best at while obtaining the services of a hot-water-heater specialist. This is a win-win situation. God demonstrates the importance of this concept through the science of ecology.

Ecology 101[1]

Ecology is the study of the relationship of organisms to their physical environment and to one another. We call its basic unit the ecosystem. An ecosystem can be as small as a tidal pool or a rotting log and as large as an ocean or a continent-spanning forest. Each ecosystem consists of a community of plants and animals in an environment that supplies them with raw materials for life. The energy necessary for all life processes reaches the earth in the form of sunlight. Green plants convert light energy into chemical energy through photosynthesis while carbon dioxide and water are transformed into sugar and stored in the plant. Herbivorous animals acquire some of the stored energy by eating the plants; those animals become food for predatory animals. Humans eat it all. These "food chains" actually overlap many times, forming elaborate webs. The chemical materials extracted from the environment and expanded into living tissue by plants and animals are continually recycled within the ecosystem through processes like photosynthesis, respiration, nitrogen fixation, and nitrification. There is a carbon cycle, an oxygen cycle, a nitrogen cycle, and a water cycle.

Relationship and Community
The first thing we notice about ecology is that it is all about rela-

tionship — to the environment and to one another — and community. In case you have not noticed, God is entirely about relationship — to your environment, which includes money, and to one another — and community.

Raw Materials for Life

A raw material is a material that needs to be processed to be of any use. Did you hear that? The environment provides raw materials — things that need to be processed for life to exist in its proper form. Likewise, God presents us with raw materials (the earth, His Spirit, our spirits, our minds, and our bodies) to live life in its proper form. Life is the very essence of what God is and He gives us raw tools to use to access that life.

Necessary Energy for Life

This notion intrigues me. The study of ecology reveals that a necessary energy is required for life to exist in the natural world. On earth, that necessary energy comes in the form of sunlight. This should make your spiritual ears perk up. See, even though you have the raw materials, you still require a necessary energy to produce life. That necessary energy is the Word of God. How many people know Jesus was the Light of the world (Gen. 1:3, John 1:4)? How many people know that we are now the light of the world (Matthew 5:14, Ephesians 5:8)? The Word of God is central to living life in abundance.

Cycles

In simple terms, the partnership cycle never stops. Each organism in the system persistently feeds the other organisms with that which it specializes in. This is a critical lesson right here. We talk about it all the time. We have cool names for it like networking, teamwork, and synergy. A lot of God's people are still living well below God's intentions because they don't live according to the principle of partnership. Our locust friends have no clearly defined ruler yet their partnership is powerful.

Defining Partnership

The dictionary defines a partner as one that shares. The suffix -*ship,* means state, condition, or quality. It follows that partnership is the state, condition, and quality of giving and receiving. Many of us like the receiving part, but falter on the giving part. As we learned in studying the attitude of God about money, God has established a give first then receive system. As a matter of fact, God basically says, "When you give I am obligated to make sure you receive." This is paramount to understanding the principle of partnership. We should not share with others with the expectation that they will pay us back with some type of favor later. We must continue to share our specialties with those who need it. God ensures that others (not necessarily those you share with) share their specialties with you when you need them.

Partners from the Start

In Genesis God only proclaimed one thing to be not good. Gen. 2:18 says, "And the Lord God said, 'It is not good that the man should be alone; I will make him an help meet for him.'" Recall that God first brought the animals before Adam so he could make a choice. Adam had enough God-given sense to know that none of the animals were appropriate for developing a proper relationship, which actually requires unity. Let us draw out the salient points of this sequence of events.

Not Good

The first two chapters in Genesis tell us everything God expects us to be now that He has restored us to our proper place in Him. The word *good* means right. How many people know that *good* comes from *God* and God is always right? God said it was not right for Adam to be alone. Notice this does not mean lonely. What does that tell us about ourselves? God did not create us to be alone — we need other people to have a fully functioning community.

Create versus Make

Create means to make something new. Make means to bring into being by forming, shaping, or altering material. In Gen. 1:26-27, God had already created male and female. When it came time to put them in the earth, God formed one male man out of the dust and blew the breath of life into him. God then took existing material out of Adam — a side — and made the woman (or man with a womb). How profound is that?

Every One Has a Purpose

All of us bring unique vantage points and experiences to any given situation. God set it up that way. God is all about interdependence. The Bible clearly tells us the female man was made for him (the male man). *For* is used as a function word to indicate purpose. Consequently, the purpose of the female man is to be the male man's "help meet."

Help Meet

Help means to assist, which means to give support (to keep from failing, yielding, or losing courage). *Help* also means to aid (to provide with what is useful or necessary in achieving an end). *Meet* means precisely adapted to a particular situation, need, or circumstance. So the role of the physical male man's "help meet" is to keep the male man from failing, yielding, and losing courage, as well as to provide him with what is useful and necessary to do what God told mankind to do, which is to be fruitful, multiply, replenish, and subdue in the earth. The female man was custom designed to "meet" the male man's needs and vice-versa. How many people know that sin came in the earth because both of the Adams stepped out of the role God gave them? The female man was supposed to keep the male man from yielding, not entice him to yield. The male man was supposed to protect his wife from improper influences and any harm or danger, not allow Satan to sweet talk his woman.

Now we have the female man, precisely adapted and adaptable to keep the male man on task. We also have the male man, who is charged with providing for, sustaining, nourishing, and protecting the female man. Mankind was now fully equipped to perform the assignment given to them by God in Gen. 1:28. Notice they are still both named Adam. There is no Eve. They are different, but still all one. They are of the same breath or spirit. They are of the same bones and flesh. All other physical males and females would come out of the union of Adam. They were partners from the start.

The Power of Partnership

Gen. 11:1-9 "And the whole earth was of one language, and of one speech. And it came to pass, as they journeyed from the east, that they found a plain in the land of Shinar; and they dwelt there. And they said one to another, Go to, let us make brick, and burn them throughly. And they had brick for stone, and slime had they for mortar. And they said, Go to, let us build us a city and a tower, whose top [may reach] unto heaven; and let us make a name, lest we be scattered abroad upon the face of the whole earth. And the Lord came down to see the city and the tower, which the children of men builded. And the Lord said, Behold, the people [is] one, and they have all one language; and this they begin to do: and now nothing will be restrained from them, which they have imagined to do. Go to, let us go down, and there confound their language, that they may not understand one another's speech. So the Lord scattered them abroad from thence upon the face of all the earth: and they left off to build the city. Therefore is the name of it called Babel; because the Lord did there confound the language of all the earth: and from thence did the Lord scatter them abroad upon the face of all the earth."

The Context

We find this series of events taking place a few generations after The Great Flood when God wiped out the entire human race saving only Noah and his family. The group of people whom this passage is referring to actually had a leader by the name of Nimrod (Gen. 10:9-10). Nimrod was Noah's great-great-grandson.

The Power of One

Everyone was of "one language." They were also of "one speech," meaning within their language they were united regarding what words they used. We call that being on the same page. In America, we all use the English language, but as we go from neighborhood to neighborhood and city to city we find not everyone uses the same speech. Can we see why there is a lack of unity in our country?

A City and a Tower

As they were in common unity with one another, they decided to make a city and a tower. They prepared a plan and went to work. Sound familiar? They then went a step further and decided they were going to "make a name" for themselves. In other words, they were going to dominate these earthly resources and establish some authority in the earth. This sounds exactly like what God created man to do in the first place. Right? Not quite.

The Lord's Reaction

The Lord observed that the people were one and nothing could restrain their capabilities. Do you see the power of partnership? The Lord then speaks to the rest of the trinity and purposes to confound the language of the people. Notice that the language of the people precipitated the unity. Good communication resulted in unity.

Confounded the Languages

There is much speculation about why God mixed up the languages. The answer is right within the text: that they may not understand one another's words. God knows that with understanding people can achieve any goal they set. With imaginations unchecked by the Holy Spirit, mankind would have quickly destroyed the earth and continued to try to "make a name" for himself. God had to end that before it started. God created man to understand His vision for mankind — thereby allowing mankind to successfully fulfill his purpose. The understanding takes place through the Word by the Holy Spirit. Without the Holy Spirit to guide them, the motivations of Nimrod and his team were not aligned with an understanding of the Word of God. The Word of God declares that mankind was created for the express purposes of God — that God's name might be magnified in the earth. Unfortunately, many of us are building cities and towers to "make a name" for ourselves among the children of men. That is essentially why some of us still do not have a handle on the money resource.

Unity is the Father's paramount concern. With the Holy Spirit now freely given to those that believe in Christ, mankind is now equipped to be unified and dominate the resources of the earth according to God's instructions. In fact, we see the theme of unity play out in Acts 1 and 2 during the time of Pentecost. Unity had to be in place for the Holy Spirit to show up, and God, in effect, restored the unity of language by breaking down the communication barriers among the disparate people of the world.

The Real Lord's Prayer

We often hear the prayer pattern that Jesus gave to His disciples (Our Father, which art in heaven...) referred to as the Lord's Prayer. Well, the Lord never prayed that prayer. He gave it to His disciples to pray. In John 17, we find a prayer Jesus actually prayed just before He was to be crucified on the cross for the sins of the world. Do you want to know what the core of it was? After praying to strengthen Himself, He began to pray for the ministry of His disciples of that time. We pick up after He prayed for the disciples.

> *John 17:20-23* "Neither pray I for these alone, but for them [also] which shall believe on me through their word; That they all may be one; as thou, Father, [art] in me, and I in thee, that they also may be one in us: that the world may believe that thou hast sent me. And the glory which thou gavest me I have given them; that they may be one, even as we are one: I in them, and thou in me, that they may be made perfect in one; and that the world may know that thou hast sent me, and hast loved them, as thou hast loved me."

Did you catch the theme? The word *one* was mentioned five times in those four verses. Out of all the things Jesus could have prayed for us at that time, He prayed for unity. By now, we should see God's entire system is set up to operate in unity.

Why We Need Money Partners

In my opinion, even Jesus knew He needed some money partners. One of his twelve apostles, Matthew, was a tax collector — not the most popular folks of their time. Most tax collectors in the Roman Empire were thought to be corrupt extortionists. However, one positive thing you can say about a tax collector of that time is that he had an intricate understanding of the money system. Another money partner Jesus had (though he betrayed him) was Judas Iscariot. The Bible does not give us much background on this particular Judas, but we do know he handled the money for the team. Now I may be off base, but I would not let anyone handle my money that did not have an understanding of how money works!

We, too, need money partners — certified public accountants, chartered financial analysts, certified financial planners, bankers, real estate experts, and entrepreneurs — people who have demonstrated competency with the money resource. Mind you, not everyone that carries these titles is qualified to offer sound financial advice. That takes us back to not believing every thing you hear. The first test is to make sure their advice agrees with the principles of the Word of God. If it passes that test, then consult some other money partners to see if the advice makes sense. Ask those money experts about their own finances. Ask them how other people who have heeded their advice are faring with their finances. If you do not know money, find someone who does.

SEEDS FOR YOUR SOIL

Partnership as a Foundation: Genesis 2

1. God started all human relationships with a family. What does that tell us about how God feels about partnership? How should we feel about partnership?

Power of Partnership: Gen. 11:1-11 and John 17

1. In Gen. 11:1-11, what did partnership allow the people to do? What implication does that have for mankind?

2. In the Lord's prayer, Jesus repeatedly talked about the concept of being one. Why do you think that is? How does that suggest we should approach the issues of life, particularly money?

God Requires Partnership: Ephesians 2, 3, and 4

1. What are the highlights of Ephesians 2 and how do they relate to partnership?

2. In Ephesians 3, we learn some things about how believers relate to Christ. How does this drive home the importance of partnership?

3. Using the example of a physical body, Ephesians 4 emphasizes the theme of partnership. Explain how the human body is a partnership example. How does this relate to the body of Christ? How does this relate to our approach to the money resource?

CHAPTER 10

EXECUTION!
EXECUTION!
EXECUTION!

Why God Believes in Productivity

The Crux of the Matter

The first thing God told us to do was to be productive. We can interpret that as God saying, "Make yourself useful!" Ever heard that from a parent? Our Father demands we be of use to Him. As we think about the fundamental concepts of preparation, prudence, and partnership, we should recognize they all require us to actually do something. It only makes sense that becoming productive is a necessary component in reestablishing a secure financial foundation and achieving financial freedom. The beauty of our spider friend is her willingness to get to work.

> *Prov. 30:28* "The spider taketh hold with her hands, and is in kings' palaces."

The Measure of Productivity

The key to mastering productivity is to understand exactly what we are called to be productive in. Consequently, productivity is tied up in understanding God's purpose for your life. This chapter is not about producing money. (There are some simple ways to produce money: open up a business or get a job!) We find what Jesus had to say about productivity in the parable of the sower, which you can read in Matthew 13, Mark 4, or Luke 8. This is a quick synopsis. A sower sowed some seed. The seed fell on four types of ground: the wayside, rocky ground, thorny ground, and good ground. The type of ground on which the seed fell determined the result of the seed.

The Lord goes on to explain that the seed represents the Word of God and the four types of ground represent types of people. The waysiders hear the Word of God declared, but the devil steals the Word that was sown in their minds before they can believe and be delivered from sin. Our rocky folks are those that hear the Word every Sunday and shout, "That's right preacher!" However, these people don't meditate on the Word for themselves so the seed cannot take root. As a result, they are easily enticed by temptation. The thorny crew hears the Word and then goes out to face life. Unfortunately, they begin to focus their attention on the external splendor of life. The Bible declares they are literally choked with the cares, riches, and pleasures of life. The good grounders hear the word and obey the word, which leads to productivity.

What can we glean from that parable? The difference between productivity and lack of productivity is the difference between obeying the Word and not obeying the Word. The waysiders, rocky folks, and thorny crew all lacked the willingness to rely on the Word of God. God measures productivity according to our ability to obey the Word of God. Mankind was actually created to receive instructions from God internally through the Holy Spirit. When we allow the Spirit to lead us, we can begin to step into the realm of productivity.

So, to be successful with the money resource, you must obey God's Word concerning money. That is it. There is no big mystery.

What is that Word? We revealed the two most essential components in chapter 4. Mankind must develop the mindsets of stewardship and giving. All success with money begins with stewardship and giving. You don't have to be a Christian to see that. Many wealthy people have a firm grasp on these concepts. Bill Gates gives away millions and millions of dollars every year. Now, you may think he gives money because he has the money. But he does not *have to* give his money away — no matter how much he makes. He understands the power of giving and that giving is a form of investing (see *Start Planting!*).

The Essential Element of Productivity: Faithfulness

Any time you have generated results, you will find you have exhibited faithfulness. Faithfulness is necessary to become productive. *The American Heritage Dictionary* gives some great definitions for *faithful*: adhering firmly and devotedly, as to a person, cause, or idea; loyal; having or full of faith; worthy of trust or belief; reliable; consistent with truth. In the book of Proverbs when we see the word *faithful*, it either refers to or comes from the Hebrew word *aman* (aw-man'). *Aman* means to support, to confirm, and to be faithful. Other words that are associated with *aman* are *established*, *steadfast*, *trustworthy*, and *believable*.

Let's flesh out some of the terms used in these definitions to get an even better understanding of the word *faithful*.

- Adhere — From adhere we get the word *adhesive*. An adhesive is a substance that unites or bonds. It is clingy and sticky. When it is properly applied, it does not go anywhere.
- Loyal — Loyal means steadfast in allegiance. We can also use the word *dedicated*. Again, not going anywhere.
- Full of Faith — This is simply *faithful* backwards. We have defined faith as complete trust in God, but it is not a mental state. It is a lifestyle that is demonstrated. Having faith means

exhibiting obedience by adhering to the Word of God, which came in the person of Jesus Christ.

◦ Reliable — This means being in the right place at the right time. Many of us are always in the wrong place at the wrong time. Can we be counted on to be in place when needed?

Luke 16:10-12 "He that is faithful in that which is least is faithful also in much: and he that is unjust in least is unjust also in much. If therefore ye have not been faithful in the unrighteous mammon, who will commit to your trust the true [riches]? And if ye have not been faithful in that which is another man's, who shall give you that which is your own?"

Unrighteous Mammon and True Riches

We previously examined unrighteous mammon in the context of friends. Now let's look at it in the context of faithfulness. This passage talks to us explicitly about being faithful with money. Or, better said, it is about adhering to set guidelines as they relate to the money resource. Notice the conditional statement that is attached to faithfulness with money. It basically says, "If you cannot be faithful with money, why would you expect spiritual blessings from the Father?"

Another Man's and Your Own

This concept can be understood on two levels. First, it clearly has implications on the natural level for all of us who seek to become business owners at some time. The Spirit really dealt with me on the significance of adhering to someone else's guidelines, being loyal to someone else's standards, being obedient to someone else's instructions, and assuming the outlook of someone else. Second, it clearly ties in to the notion of being a steward.

God requires faithfulness of his spiritual offspring. Rom. 8:14 reads, "For as many as are led by the Spirit of God, they are the sons of God." Well, what does it mean to be led by the Spirit of God? It simply means the actions we take are based on adherence to the teaching of the Holy Spirit. The Holy Spirit only teaches the Word of God. Therefore, the scripture declares we are only considered sons of God when we are loyal and obedient to the Spirit of God. Not everyone is God's child. Jesus had to clear this up with the Pharisees and the scribes in John 8:44. He said, "You are of your father the devil because you do what he does." What does the devil do? He leans unto his own understanding. The Spirit of God does not lead him. He is led by out-sight.

Productivity is Hard to Find

Prov. 20:6 "Most men will proclaim every one his own goodness: but a faithful man who can find?"

The Good News Bible translates this verse as, "Everyone talks about how loyal and faithful he is, but just try to find someone who really is!" I have always liked this verse, but I like it even better in this version. It takes me back to a statistic I read in *Fortune* magazine a little while ago: 20 percent of the people in the United States control 80 percent of the natural wealth in the United States. What is interesting is you can apply what people have dubbed the 80/20 rule to almost any situation in the world. Let's start with the local ministries each of us are currently or may have ever been involved in. Is it safe to say 20 percent of the people do 80 percent of the work? What about fraternities and sororities? Is it safe to say 20 percent of the people do 80 percent of the work? What about on your job? Is it safe to say on a team project 20 percent of the people do 80 percent of the work? School? Volunteer efforts? Sports teams?

Has anyone ever heard the phrase the faithful few? What about this phrase: Many are called, but few are chosen. Few people are faithful enough to be chosen as a son of God. God's call on our lives is to be a righteous example of Him. We do that by adhering to the teaching of the Spirit of God. God calls every member of mankind to a life of righteousness, but there are few people who decide to live a life that is full of faith and solely dependent on God. Faithfulness actually leads to productivity. Even in the production of money, the principle of faithfulness applies. Wealthy people continue to grow wealthier because they have found approaches that work and are faithful to those approaches.

Redefining Work

Work is God's word for productivity. But productivity is often not what we think of when we hear the word *work*. When we think of work we often think of the place we spend most of our time during the week so we can collect our paychecks. God's idea of work can encompass that time, but I would argue that for many of us it does not. *Merriam Webster's Collegiate Dictionary* gives some definitions of work that completely line up with God's idea of work. *Work*: to exert oneself physically or mentally in sustained effort for a purpose; to function or operate according to a plan or design; to make way slowly and with difficulty.

Sustained Effort for a Purpose

Can you pick out the key word in our first definition? God wants our everyday effort to reflect His unique purpose for our lives. God does not do anything without a reason and He would prefer us to operate in the same manner. Purpose is an essential element of work. Without purpose we are not working. We are wasting time.

According to a Plan

The only way to discover the plan God has for you is to communicate with God. We must develop a daily prayer life that consists of talking to God and listening for God's voice and instructions. Think of it as your daily one-to-one with the boss. It is an exchange. You talk. God talks back.

Slowly and with Difficulty

Work takes patience and perseverance. Anyone that is looking for a quick fix to his or her financial doldrums is in for a rude awakening. That person has a warped sense of work.

As we learn more about God's outlook on work be aware that it takes money to do God's work. However, God's emphasis is not on the money. His emphasis is on the work. The purpose and the plan come from Him. Mankind does the work. He did all the work He planned to do on days one through six. On day seven, He rested and left the rest of the development of the earth up to mankind. This development takes place slowly and with difficulty.

God's Attitude about Work

What is the first thing God did with the man He created? The first thing God told man to do was "dress the garden and keep it." In simple terms, He told man to get to work. Why? God is a working God. He created us in His image and after His likeness. Through work we find out what we are capable of accomplishing. In other words, there is no way to maximize the potential within us without doing some work. James put it this way in James 2:26, "Faith without works is dead!" There is no way to exercise faith if you are not doing any work. Let's take a look at a segment of the second letter to the Thessalonians, written by Paul, Silvaneus, and Timothy.

2 Thess. 3:10-11 "For even when we were with you, this

we commanded you, that if any would not work, neither should he eat. For we hear that there are some
which walk among you disorderly, working not at all,
but are busybodies."

No Work, No Eat

This is a tough stance for most Christians to embrace. Through the
Holy Spirit, the men of God proclaim that if one does not work, he
should not eat. First, we must understand this was written to an assembly of purported followers of Christ. As a follower of Christ, we
are to be about our Father's business, that is, we should be working.
When we are not working we should not expect to partake in the
fruit of the ministry — the grace, joy, peace, favor, faith, prosperity,
and so forth.

Disorderly

When we think of the word *disorderly*, we often think chaotic or
rowdy. We should think of disorderly in more simplistic terms: without a proper plan. God established a divine order for mankind to
walk in. This order includes a four-letter word — work! Many of us
are following our own plan and do not realize that we are the very
ones that are disorderly.

Busybodies

We know that God's definition of work includes these elements:
purpose, plan, and challenges. Many of us give the appearance of
working, but essentially we are just disorderly busybodies. Work, as
God defines it, goes far beyond doing good deeds. It goes far beyond
attaining a title or position in an assembly of Christians. It goes far
beyond gaining promotion after promotion on our jobs. The only
work God accepts is the work He has given us to do. Many Christians want credit because they sing in the choir, gave a big offering

last year, volunteer at the shelter once a quarter, lead this and that ministry, or sit in the third row every Sunday. They are screaming, "Look God! See all the stuff I am doing because I love Jesus." God's only response is, "Is that what I told you to do?" Plenty of people are running around doing stuff God did not tell them to do. They are busybodies that are "working not at all." Most people would define it as work, but God does not.

What happens to a person when he or she does not eat? After a while, he or she dies. In other words, when we are not working, God basically says we might as well die. Many of us think that because we are generating income God is satisfied. We fail to realize that God's work is not about generating income. It is about changing minds. When we go about changing minds, income follows.

The Link Between Work and Destiny

It is important to work and not to be a busybody because your work leads you into your destiny. As one of my brothers in the ministry often says, "Your work is just an assignment or series of assignments that leads to your destiny." To put it in perspective, busybodies are simply hindering their meeting with destiny. You see, I am working right now. This book is part of my life's work. I love to write. *Stop Digging!* is one of my assignments as God continues to reveal my destiny to me. Even in my job, I am working and not just at going to a job. I work in investments, which is directly linked to this book series and even more directly linked to the vision God has given me concerning financial deliverance for the true body of Christ.

God does want us to be busy. He just doesn't want us to be busybodies. When we examine the word *business* what do we notice? It looks a lot like the word *busyness*. God is, in fact, calling for busyness instead of busybody-ness. The former means you are doing the work God created you to do — busyness is synonymous with work. The latter means you are doing stuff you created for you to do —

being disorderly. It is a subtle difference because we often confuse the good things we do with the purpose God created us for. I'm not suggesting you stop doing good things for people. This is an exhortation to make sure you are doing your work while you are doing what you consider to be good things!

God did not create us to drift from job to job searching for the next stream of fixed income. God equipped us with creativity and diversity that lends itself to the ability to generate multiple sources of variable income in perpetuity. Many of us are stuck on this month-to-month, "I just want to make it" approach when God is trying to show us something much larger and more comprehensive. Has anyone ever read about the virtuous woman in Proverbs 31? This lady had at least nine different sources of income. Nine!!

What the Bible Says about Work

> *Prov. 23:4* "Labour not to be rich: cease from thine own wisdom."

Labor Not to Be Rich?
Many people teach this verse to support the misconstrued perception that Christians should not want to be rich. God is concerned about the believer's focus, not whether he or she is rich. This verse really tells us to stop relying on our own wisdom. In other words, work should begin with reliance on the Wisdom of God.

> *Prov. 16:3* "Commit thy works unto the Lord, and thy thoughts shall be established."

Commit Thy Works
Many of us are just plain not committed to the work God has for us. We have our own plans and ideas about what our work situation

should look like. That word *commit* is tied up in the concept of trusting God. This verse tells us when we truly submit our spirit, soul, and body to the Lord our thoughts are established. This is a two-step process. God begins to feed you His desires for your life. Then, as you implement those thoughts that are aligned with the works of God, the substance or essence of your thoughts begins to manifest in the natural realm. Your vision — because it's God's vision — becomes reality right before your eyes.

> *Prov. 14:23* "In all labour there is profit: but the talk of the lips [tendeth] only to penury."

Profit or Penury

Profit, in this context, means productivity. *Penury* is talking about poverty or uselessness. Many people suffer from a lack of productivity — that is, poverty — and do not know it because they are busybodies and have fooled themselves into thinking they are doing a great work for God. Talk is cheap. So are vain works. Vain works are the equivalent of the "talk of the lips" because they are not based on instructions from the Boss. You talked yourself into doing it. Poverty is a choice. The scriptures support such an understanding. Minister Shundrawn explores this in chapter 3 of *Start Planting!*

> *Prov. 12:11* "He that tilleth his land shall be satisfied with bread: but he that followeth vain *persons is* void of understanding."

Vain =Void

This proverb supports the verses we examined from Thessalonians. I've italicized the phrase "persons is" for a reason. If you drop the italicized words, the verse literally reads, "He that follows vain void of understanding." This is not referring to following vain people *per se.* To me it is saying that the person who works his own works is not a person who understands the plan and purpose of God.

> *Prov. 14:4* "Where no oxen [are], the crib [is] clean: but much increase [is] by the strength of the ox."

The Ox

This became one of my favorite proverbs when God finally revealed to me what He is talking about. The crux of it: You have to do the dirty work in order for wealth to manifest in your life. See, when you have no oxen, you do have a clean stall but you do not make any money because you cannot work the field. The only way to plow the land is to own oxen. Now let's relate the story to us. When we do not study the Word of God we can live a comfortable life because we are fine with what we are doing. However, the only way to develop a personal relationship with God and find out your destiny is through the revelation of the Word by the Holy Spirit. We will never make it into the wealthy place — spiritually and naturally — if we are not willing to change according to the Word of God.

God wants us to seek His purpose for our lives. The problem is He doesn't usually drop it on us all at one time. Instead, He gives us a series of assignments (work) that lead us in the way of destiny. Those assignments require serious change. After all, if we could get where God intends for us to go by doing what we are doing, what would we need God for?

Take a close look at yourself. Are there any areas of your life that you have yet to relinquish to God? For many of us, that area is finances. Many of us have carved out our own agendas based on past experiences and what other people think and say. We have yet to ask God whether our agenda is aligned with His agenda. Let me reveal a secret: true success in not necessarily in our personal agenda. We can fight with that conclusion or learn to accept it and begin to align our agenda with God's. That requires productivity. So let's *Stop Digging!* and *Start Planting!*. In other words, let's go to work!

Seeds for Your Soil

Understanding Productivity: Matthew 13, Mark 4, and Luke 8

1. Is making money the indicator of productivity? If not, then what is? How does this affect the believer's attitude and approach to making money?

Faithfulness: Luke 16:1-12

1. Explain the link between faithfulness and the ability to be productive. Why are the two notions related? How does this apply to our money management methodology?

Understanding Work: 2 Thessalonians 3 and James 2

1. Describe God's definition and attitude toward work as portrayed in 2Thessalonians 3.

2. Describe the interaction between faith and works. What does that mean for us who think that money is going to fall out of the sky?

PART IV

APPENDICES

Prepare to Start Planting!

Practical Ways to Institute Financial Order in Your Life

Step I — Review & Self-Assessment
The Stop Digging! Review (20 Things I Learned)

1. Mankind was created to produce, increase, replenish, and subdue in the earth.

2. The earth does not belong to mankind. It belongs to God.

3. Mankind is established as the steward of the earth.

4. God has a destiny for each of us individually and for mankind collectively.

5. Money is merely a universal resource in the earth.

6. God is concerned about our relationship with money, not money itself.

7. Debt is the polar opposite of God's nature and is the result of a lack of discipline.

8. Cosigning is another form of bad debt.

9. The root of debt is the lack of a relationship with the Holy Spirit.

10. There is a real and direct link between that which the believer meditates on and his or her financial situation.

11. Stewardship is a necessary mindset for financial freedom to manifest in one's life.

12. Giving is a necessary mindset for financial freedom to manifest in one's life.

13. Spiritual in-sight must replace natural out-sight for the believer to successfully navigate the world of personal finance.

14. The dominion that mankind has been given in the earth is displayed through the use of words.

15. The proper mindset and a God-like use of words leads to a behavioral transformation.

16. Reaching financial freedom is dependent upon the believer's willingness to be obedient to the Word of God.

17. Preparation is a fundamental factor in financial freedom.

18. Prudence is a fundamental factor in financial freedom.

19. Partnering is a fundamental factor in financial freedom.

20. Productivity is not only essential to financial freedom, it is the end goal of the believer's life.

The Stop Digging! Assessment

1. I have a mortgage.
   ○ Yes   ○ No

2. I have consumer debt.
   ○ Yes   ○ No

3. I have educational debt.
   ○ Yes   ○ No

4. I have other debts (this includes auto loans).
   ○ Yes   ○ No

5. I know the difference between an asset and a liability.
   ○ Yes   ○ No

6. I know what my immediate financial obligations are.
   ○ Yes   ○ No

7. I have a budget.
   ○ Yes   ○ No

8. I have a financial plan.
   ○ Yes   ○ No

9. I have adequately planned for my dependents and/or other family and/or my household.
   ○ Yes   ○ No

10. I have adequately planned for my latter years.
    ○ Yes   ○ No

11. I have adequately planned out my estate.
    ○ Yes   ○ No

12. I invest on a regular basis.
    ○ Yes   ○ No

Give yourself one (1) point for each No in Questions 1-4 and one (1) point for each Yes in Questions 5-12.

A score of 9-12 means you are ready to *Start Planting!*. You will greatly benefit from the principles and strategies outlined in Minister Shundrawn's book. Don't forget to examine the areas in which you did not score a point.

A score of 6-8 means you probably need to review *Stop Digging!* and definitely examine the areas in which you did not score a point. *Start Planting!* will begin to take you to another level in personal finance, but to maximize the benefits of the series, you must shore up your financial foundation.

A score of 0-5 means you must reexamine the principles laid out in *Stop Digging!* and begin to apply them to your life. *Start Planting!* will be a great read for you. However, you must plug up the hole in the ground and prepare your soil properly.

Anyone who scored less than nine should consult our reading list in *Start Planting!* Specifically, I recommend you read *Personal Finance for Dummies* by Eric Tyson and *Rich Dad, Poor Dad* by Robert Kiyosaki. Both of these books are easy reads and will introduce you to practical approaches to understanding and managing money. Mr. Tyson's book gives you an idea of all the different things you can do with your money and what may make sense for you. In Step III of this exercise, you will get a small glimpse of what it has to offer. Mr. Kiyosaki's book offers readers a peek into his personal story and teaches how to decipher between transactions that create wealth and those that destroy wealth.

Step II — Calculate Net Worth
The Concept of Net Worth: Owns and Owes
In a nutshell net worth is all that you own (assets) less all that you owe (liabilities). There is just a one-letter difference between positive net worth and negative net worth. For practical purposes, let us classify the *owns* and the *owes*. Now, of course, some *owns* are better than others just as some *owes* are more essential than others. When we talk about owning versus owing, we are speaking of the

Net Worth	
OWN	**OWE**
Business ownership	Car lease
Car payments	Clothing
Fine Art	Credit Cards
Investments (stocks, bonds, etc.)	Entertainment
Mortgage payments	Food
Retirement plans	Gifts
Whole life insurance	Monthly expenses (bills)
	Term insurance
	Vacations
Adapted from *Smart Money Moves for African-Americans*, by Kelvin Boston.	

difference between investment and consumption. To break it down to the very essence of this book series, we are discussing the difference between planting and digging. Okay...so what is an investment? An *investment* is defined as property or another possession acquired for future financial return or benefit. And what is consumption? *Consumption* is the using up of purchased goods or services.

So when we plant, we fully expect to reap future returns and benefits. We put our energy into acquiring property and possessions that exhibit those qualities. On the contrary, when we dig we cancel our future and at the end of the day we have nothing to show for our hard work.

Please note that everything called an investment is not necessarily a good investment. Some items that we have listed under the *owns* category actually act more like liabilities than assets. For example, car payments represent a path to ownership, but most people with financial sense will tell you that buying a car on credit is a horrible financial investment. Why? Well, you pay more than the car is worth over a period of time (for most people three to five years). Moreover, as soon as you drive the car off the lot, it is worth substantially less than the sticker price (let alone what you actually end up paying for it). Lastly, because you are making payments you have locked up a portion of your future income every month so you have now limited your financial flexibility. What are ways to avoid this dilemma? Pay cash for your cars. Instead of buying a new car, buy a two- or three-year-old car with low miles. If you feel like you must borrow, take out a home equity loan to pay for the car and get the tax benefit while you make payments (make sure you pay off in three years or less). A more controversial claim that I mentioned in chapter 3 is that having mortgage payments is not always a good investment. Again, we must examine the financial foundation on which we are stacking the financial responsibility of home ownership.

What the Word Says about Net Worth

Prov. 13:22 "A good [man] leaveth an inheritance to his children's children: and the wealth of the sinner [is] laid up for the just."

God's child is all about asset gathering and wealth creation. He or she understands the importance of abundant living right now and in the generations to come. He or she values the concept of building for the future. He or she is not selfish. Through his or her obedience to God, he or she preserves many generations through examples and teaching. He or she perpetuates "net worth" champions. Before we get all happy, it is important to understand a couple of things. Here we go...

Good

In this context, *good* means bountiful, kind, gracious, and wealthy. These are the attributes of God. These attributes are given to the born again believer once he or she accepts Christ. It does not stop there, however. The believer must live his or her life according to the principles of the Word of God as directed by the Holy Spirit. Notice this does not mean do some good things in the community and attend church every Sunday. What makes one "good" is his or her willingness to obey God, not do "good" things.

Sinner

This is specifically referring to those who continue in sin and do not have a covenant relationship with God. Recall the only way to develop a relationship with God is through the Holy Spirit, which is a gift to the born again believer.

Laid Up

"Laid up" does not mean we do not have to do any work. "Laid up" means it is ready for the taking, but we have to operate according to the will of God.

Rom. 8:14 tells us as many as are led by the Spirit they are the sons of God. Did anybody pick up the qualifications of being considered "good" in God's eyes? One must be led by the Spirit in order be a "good man." The Spirit leads us to obey the Word of God.

Net Worth Worksheet

We all need to know our net worth. The following categorizations will help you to assess your net worth.

Property Assets
Residence   _____
Vacation Home   _____
Furnishings   _____
Automobiles   _____
Art, jewelry, other valuables   _____
Equity Assets
Stocks   _____
Equity mutual funds   _____
Variable annuities   _____
Limited partnerships   _____
Rental real estate   _____
Business interests   _____
Fixed Assets
U.S. Gov't bonds   _____
Municipal bonds   _____
Corporate bonds   _____
Face amount certificates   _____
Fixed-dollar annuities   _____

Other fixed assets _____

Cash Reserve Assets

Checking accounts _____

Savings accounts _____

Money-market funds _____

Certificates of deposit _____

Other cash reserve accounts _____

Total Assets _____

Liabilities

Home mortgage _____

Other mortgage _____

Automobile loans _____

Bank loans _____

Personal loans _____

Credit card debt _____

Other debts _____

Total Liabilities _____

NET WORTH _____

(assets minus liabilities)

Based on a concept found in the *Dummies* book, let's measure your financial state.

- Feverish — Net worth is less than half your household's annual income.
- Functional — Net worth is more than half your household's annual income, but less than a five years income
- Fruitful — Net worth is more than five years income.

When I first did this calculation I realized that I had some serious work to do. Please join me on the journey from Feverish to Fruitful! Preparation, prudence, partnering, and productivity are the essential components to reaching fruitfulness. Set that goal and do not give up. Do not dig up the seeds.

Step III — Establish a Debt-Cancellation/ Spending-Reduction Plan
Debt Cancellation

This discussion is based on principles from *Personal Finance for Dummies*.

Saving While in Debt

Generally, it is a bad idea to save while you are in debt, particularly when we are dealing with consumer debt and automobile loans. Consumer debt is priced at enormous interest rates — usually 13 percent and above annually. The stock market has returned around 10 percent annually on average. Now, it doesn't take a rocket scientist to see the bad math there. Paying down high interest debt with savings is akin to giving yourself an investment return equal to the interest that would be accruing on your balance monthly (sometimes daily). Remember opportunity cost? If you have some mortgage debt and or some educational debt it *may* make sense to invest in other investment vehicles as you carry that debt, but it all depends on the interest rates involved. When in doubt, seek professional partners. Sound familiar?

Hey Buddy! I Have No Savings

Listen, I have been there and done that too. Hang in there, that is why we'll get to the spending issue shortly. A technique that my wife used was to transfer her high interest debt to cards with temporary zero percent offers. The method saved her hundreds of dollars in interest while allowing her to methodically and faithfully demolish her mountain of consumer debt. The *Dummies* book also suggests trading in cards with annual fees for cards with no fees, as well as trading in high interest cards for cards with lower interest rates.

Scissors R' Us

Another technique that my wife reluctantly implemented (with my urging of course) was to move from many cards to two. Now she is down to one. She let her scissors do the talking then promptly called each credit card company to cancel her accounts. Now we pay cash for everything. We use cards for points and convenience. We are big believers in the debit card phenomenon.

Miscellaneous Techniques

Here are a few additional suggestions for gaining control of your consumer debt: decrease the amount of borrowing ability you have; avoid all retailing cards; leave your cards at home when you go out; avoid purchasing depreciating assets on credit; and shun the minimum and monthly payment mentalities.

Spending Reduction

There is a stunning revelation in *The Millionaire Next Door*: most millionaires live well below their means. I have an equally stunning one — okay, so it's really just an opinion: most broke people live way above their means. In other words, people with financial issues typically spend too much.

Where's the Budget?

The main reason most people spend too much is because they have no standard for comparison. What is the definition of *too much*? Of course, that answer depends on how much income you generate and what financial goals you have in place. The budget falls out of that analysis.

Credit Card Management

Why am I mentioning this again? Because it is the greatest enabler of the digger mentality. Order your credit reports from the three major bureaus: Equifax (www.equifax.com), Trans Union (www.transunion.com), and Experian (www.experian.com). Studies have found that the majority of credit reports have incorrect information on them. Therefore, as you manage your credit, it is prudent to know what specific information credit grantors consider when making financing decisions. The credit bureaus also provide consumers with credit scores and tips on how to improve them.

Food, Food and More Food

Many of us would be shocked at the amount of money we spend on food. If you do not already know, you'll find out in the next section. There are several simple ways to reduce spending on food, including taking a lunch daily, buying in bulk, and actively monitoring dining out.

Shop-a-holics and Their Habitation

If you have problem with shopping, stay away from people who like to shop and stay away from where they live — the mall. Got it?

Vacations

Maybe you really cannot afford to go on two vacations a year. Maybe you need to cut it to one. Maybe you need to go every other year. Maybe you cannot afford to be as extravagant as you would like to be. Maybe you can only be extravagant every three years. Maybe you need to investigate less expensive alternatives. Whatever the case may be, you must take a realistic look at your vacation spending relative to our financial needs and goals.

Cars

The Millionaire Next Door reveals that only 23.5 percent of millionaires own a car that is the current year's model and nearly 37 percent purchase used cars. Millionaires spend less than 1 percent of their net worth on vehicles. Broke people? 30 percent! Furthermore, 80 percent of millionaires buy instead of lease. Think before you sink a significant portion of your monthly income (car note plus new car insurance) into a depreciating asset.

Clothes

I like to look good. I love fine designers — from Giorgio Armani to Valentino to Joseph Abboud — but I buy almost exclusively on sale. And I only pay cash (or I use my charge card for the points). Clothes are fun and essential, but we must have a grip on the money that we spend on clothes relative to the money we generate and our financial priorities. My wife finds cashmere and wool winter coats for less than five dollars at the thrift store. These coats are of high quality and someone probably paid hundreds of dollars for them just a few years ago. There are bargains to be had. Do you search for them?

Step IV — Prepare for Financial Planning

Budgeting 101
Meet our budgeting case studies.

- Martha Shopper — Martha has a propensity to shop, which is fine. However, she tends to spend money she does not have.
- Ruth Parent — Ruth is a single mother who is trying to manage her household.
- Mike and Delilah Couple — The Couples have been married for two years and are planning for the future.
- Joe and Rachel Family — Joe and Rachel live the American

Dream. They have two-and-a-half kids, a dog, a mortgage, and a car note.

⚫ John Excessive — Mr. Excessive has a nice job and likes nice things. The problem is John cannot really afford to buy every single thing he likes. Unfortunately, that does not stop him.

What do all of these people have in common? They need a budget. Budgeting is not as bad as we make it out to be, but it does require some work. Budgets should not and do not have to be stringent, but they should be monitored and managed faithfully. There are several types of budgets. Some people put themselves on a savings budget in which they force themselves to save a certain amount of money every month before they pay bills. Others prefer a spending budget in which they allocate a certain amount of money to major expenses and divvy up the rest as they see fit. Then you have a group of people (like me) who are anal and create a line item budget. Whatever type you choose, just remember that all budgets should be flexible.

Let's take a closer look at some financial situations.

Martha Shopper's Profile
⚫ Monthly net income: $2,000
⚫ Rent: $850
⚫ Student loans (interest only): $200
⚫ Car note: $350
⚫ Credit card interest: $300
⚫ Other household expenses: $500
⚫ Shopping: $300
⚫ Total monthly outflow: $2,500
⚫ Monthly deficit: −$500
⚫ Savings account balance: $500
⚫ Credit card balance (20 cards): $20,000

Martha Shopper's Treatment Plan

- Transfer credit card balances to zero interest credit cards; close accounts and cut up cards.
- Request copy of credit report to clear up any outstanding credit issues.
- Avoid the mall and places that look like the mall.
- Consider moving into a cheaper apartment or getting a roommate.
- Take money from apartment change, shopping hiatus, and savings account to methodically pay off the outstanding credit card debt.
- Reconfigure student loan to include paying down principal.
- Look for other opportunities to cut expenses.

Other household expenses include insurance, gasoline, utilities, telephone service, cable service, and internet access.

Ruth Parent's Profile

- Monthly net income: $2,500
- Rent: $800
- Child expenses: $500
- Car note: $300
- Credit card interest: $75
- Other household expenses: $600
- Shopping: $100
- Total monthly outflow: $2,375
- Monthly surplus: $125
- Savings account balance: $2,500
- Retirement balance: $7,500
- Credit card balance (7 cards): $5,000

Ruth Parent's Treatment Plan

- Transfer credit card balances to zero interest credit cards; close accounts and cut up cards.
- Request copy of credit report to clear up any outstanding credit issues.
- Take money saved from transferring balances, shopping money, and money from savings account to pay off credit cards.
- Find other opportunities to cut expenses until debt is paid off.

*Other household expenses include insurance, gasoline, utilities, telephone service, cable service, and internet access. Child expenses include care, clothing, allowance, school expenses, toys, and entertainment.

Mike and Delilah Couple's Profile

- Monthly net income: $4,250
- Mortgage related: $1,500
- Car notes: $575
- Student loans: $750
- Credit card interest: $225
- Other household expenses: $1,050
- Total monthly outflow: $4,100
- Monthly surplus: $150
- Savings account balance: $5,000
- Retirement balances: $4,500
- Credit card balance (4 cards): $12,000

Mike and Delilah Couple's Treatment Plan

- Consider buying a cheaper house. Over 40 percent of monthly income is going to house, which means the Couples probably have too much house.

- Implement credit card strategies mentioned in Martha Shopper's profile.
- Take money from decreased house expenses and eliminated credit card debt to increase contribution to retirement account and pursue other investments.

*Other household expenses include insurance, gasoline, utilities, telephone service, cable service, and internet access.

Joe and Rachel Family's Profile

- Monthly net income: $5,000
- Mortgage related: $1,650
- Children expenses: $1,500
- Car note: $350
- Credit card interest: $150
- Other household expenses: $1,450
- Total monthly outflow: $5,100
- Monthly deficit: –$100
- Savings account balance: $10,000
- Retirement balances: $50,000
- Credit card balance (10 cards): $25,000

Joe and Rachel Family's Potential Prognosis

- Consider paying down credit card debt with savings.
- Explore the option of finding a less expensive house.
- Reduce expenses to save and invest more money.

*Other household expenses include insurance, gasoline, utilities, telephone service, cable service, and internet access. Children expenses include care, clothing, allowance, school expenses, toys, and entertainment.

John Excessive's Profile
- Monthly net income: $5,000
- Condo: $2,000
- Leisure/entertainment spending: $1,500
- Shopping: $350
- Student loans: $400
- Car note: $550
- Other household expenses: $1,000
- Total monthly outflow: $5,800
- Monthly deficit: –$800
- Savings account balance: $3,000
- Investments: $5,000
- Retirement balance: $6,000
- Credit card balance (3 cards): $15,000

John Excessive's Treatment Plan
- Cut leisure spending dramatically.
- Go on a shopping diet.
- Move into a less expensive condo.
- Implement credit card strategies mentioned above.
- Direct more money to retirement funds and investments after paying off credit cards.

*Other household expenses include insurance, gasoline, utilities, telephone service, cable service, and internet access.

Have you noticed what our friends have in common? They are all violating the spiritual law of giving. They have yet to grasp the power found in the mindset of giving.

Spending Assessment
The table that follows gives us some generic categories in which to

track our monthly expenses. Before you can begin financial planning, it is critical to have a clear picture of your current income and expenses per month. I humbly implore each of my readers to spend the next month meticulously tracking where you spend your money. This will be an eye-popping experience for the majority of you but well worth the effort.

For a little perspective, consider these statistics from *Smart Money Moves for African-Americans.* The average household in America spends 13.9 percent of their income on food, 30.8 percent on housing, 5.6 percent on clothing, 16.1 percent on transportation, 4.9 percent on entertainment, 5.3 percent on healthcare, and 5.3 percent on other expenses.

Charitable Contributions

Tithes   _____

Offering   _____

Other   _____

Taxes

Social Security   _____

Federal   _____

State/Local   _____

Roof

Rent   _____

Mortgage   _____

Property Taxes   _____

Gas/electric/oil   _____

Water/garbage   _____

Stop Digging!

Phone   _____
Cable TV   _____
Furniture/appliances   _____
Maintenance/repairs   _____

Food

Supermarket   _____
Restaurants/Takeout   _____

Transportation

Gasoline   _____
Maintenance/repairs   _____
State registration fees   _____
Tolls/Parking   _____
Bus/Subway fares   _____

Style

Clothing   _____
Shoes   _____
Jewelry   _____
Dry Cleaning   _____

Debt Repayments

Credit/Charge Cards   _____
Auto Loans   _____
Student Loans   _____
Other   _____

Fun Stuff

Entertainment _____
Vacation/Travel _____

Personal Care

Haircuts _____
Health Club/Gym _____
Makeup _____
Other _____

Personal Business

Accountant _____
Attorney _____
Financial Advisor _____

Health Care

Physicians/Hospital _____
Drugs _____
Dental & Vision _____
Therapy _____

Insurance

Homeowners/Renters _____
Auto _____
Health _____
Life _____
Disability _____

Educational Expenses

Courses _____

Books _____

Supplies _____

Children

Day Care _____

Toys _____

Child Support _____

Savings & Investments

Savings _____

401(k) _____

Individual Stocks _____

Bonds _____

Stock mutual funds _____

Bond mutual funds _____

Real Estate _____

Other _____

The Basis for a Financial Plan

The following questions provide a base on which to build a successful financial plan. They will help you hone in on the some of the details of your spending habits while refocusing you on the big picture. With the answers on paper, you will be prepared to work with professional money partners to develop a game plan.

1. How much do I spend monthly?
2. How much do I budget to spend monthly?
3. What are my largest spending categories and how do they

compare to national averages?

4. What is the current state of my investment portfolio?

5. What is my current net worth?

6. What is my net worth goal in five years? Ten years? Twenty years?

Questions to Ask a Potential Financial Advisor

It is completely appropriate and prudent to investigate potential money partners. It is important to understand something about their expertise, incentives, and track record. These are questions that any potential advisor should be willing and able to answer to your satisfaction.

1. Tell me about your professional background. How and why did you get into the business of advising people on their personal finances?

2. What are your specific areas of expertise? Tax planning? Estate planning? Legal issues? Investments?

3. Help me understand how you are compensated. Is your compensation commission-based, fee-based, or a combination of both?

4. Give me the highlights of your own personal financial plan. What are some of the best decisions you have made? What are some of the worst decisions you have made?

5. Would you be willing to provide me with some references from your client base?

The Last Word

There once was a woman who made around $25,000 a year before taxes. After taxes she took home about $21,000 or $1,750 per month. On a monthly basis, she spent about $200 on lottery tickets with the desire to hit it big. Ten years later, her ship had not come in and on top of that she was laid off from her job. She had about $1,000 saved up, but that was the extent of her cash flow. What were her options? She really did not have any. She had to quickly find another job. Her cousin worked with the same company making the same salary. Her cousin was putting $200 per month into a mutual fund that gained ten percent annually on average. When the layoff notices came around, she did not panic. Why? Because she had almost $41,000 in cash stashed away in her mutual fund accounts. Needless to say, she decided to open her own business. This story is loosely based on a real-life account that a good friend shared with me concerning one of his employees. Variations on this story play out in many ways in many people's lives. Just substitute shopping, vacations, cars, food, or other items for the lottery tickets. It is imperative that we change our mindset about the money resource if we want to experience freedom and prosperity.

These two women had the exact same resources. What separated them? Mindsets. The first woman had no concept of financial freedom beyond being lucky enough to win the lottery. Many of us do not fundamentally believe we can truly be financially free without receiving some magical influx of cash. Therefore we shop, vacation, and spend some more because we might as well enjoy life now. Our results speak for themselves. We ask ourselves questions like, "How come I never have any money?" The second woman had a vision and a goal. She exhibited prudence. While her cousin was faithful to the lottery, she was faithful to working toward financial freedom. She believed that building her assets over time would give her better options for life in the future. Guess what? She was right. We must ask ourselves these important questions: What do I believe about the money resource? Do I believe what God's Word says about money? Do I believe it is possible to experience freedom and abundance as a result of my hard work? Am I content with a limited knowledge about money?

I hope this book leads to a radical change in your mindset concerning the money resource. Aside from demolishing your ignorance about the money resource, I wanted to help you establish a spiritual foundation to pursue practical, functional solutions to whatever is ailing your financial situation. I hope you're ready now to *Stop Digging!* and *Start Planting!*

ENDNOTES

Chapter 1 — I'm an Original

A. Keogh, E. "An Overview of the Science of Fingerprints." Anil Aggrawal's Internet Journal of Forensic Medicine and Toxicology, vol. 2, no. 1 (January–June) 2001. Available on the World Wide Web:

http://anil299.tripod.com/vol_002_no_001/papers/paper005.html

B. www.eyeticket.com/technology/irisrecog.html and www.retina-scan.com/retina_scan_technology.htm.

C. www.theiai.org/disciplines/odontology/

D. www.esr.cri.nz/features/esr_and_dna/whatisdna/index.htm

Chapter 2 — I Don't Know Money

E. Morris, Kenneth. *The Wall Street Journal Guide to Understanding Money and Investing.* New York: Fireside, 1999.

Chapter 6 — Changing My Approach

F. http://iridia.ulb.ac.be/~mdorigo/ACO/RealAnts.html

G. http://njnj.essortment.com/rockbadger_rhwe.htm

H. www.affa.gov.au/

I. www.bigchalk.com/cgi-bin/WebObjects/
WOPortal.woa/wa/HWCDA/file?fileid=50425&flt=ga

Chapter 9 — I'm Not an Island

J. www.infoplease.com

ABOUT THE AUTHOR

A native of Chicago, Illinois, Cliff "Tony" Goins IV is a certified public accountant and former investment professional with extensive experience in financial services. Cliff's professional career includes successful stints at American Express Financial Advisors, Smith Whiley & Company, Radio One, Inc., and Holland Capital Management, L.P. Cliff's investment views have been carried by Bloomberg News.

In the fall of 2002, Cliff and his partner, Shundrawn Thomas, founded Adelphos Holdings LLC to release to the world the gifts that God has planted in them. In their first project, each merges their knowledge base of finance and investments with the revelation of God's Word to uniquely convey to their readers and listeners God's attitude toward money and investing. The journey begins with *Stop Digging! A Spiritual Guide to Financial Freedom and Sound Stew-*

ardship and *Start Planting! A Spiritual Guide to Wealth Creation and Successful Investing.*

An active member in the community, Mr. Goins serves as a minister and as a member of the board of directors at the Look Up and Live Full Gospel Church in Chicago. To aid church members in the area of personal finance, Cliff created a life-changing economic empowerment series for the organization. Mr. Goins has also participated in and led many community service initiatives, including mentoring and tutoring elementary and high school students.

Cliff holds a bachelor of science degree in accounting from Florida A&M University. Cliff also has a master of business administration degree in finance, strategy, and marketing from the Kellogg School of Management at Northwestern University. In addition, Cliff is a candidate for Level ii of the Chartered Financial Analyst program and holds Series 7 and 66 securities licenses.

Cliff is joyfully married to the lovely and dynamic Janelle.

WHAT DO YOU THINK?

We want your input — help make our products better!

Log on to http://www.StopStartBooks.com now!
*The interface is easy and you'll receive tons of FREE
and useful information.*

Give us feedback on:

∼ Book content ∼

∼ Book relevance ∼

∼ Book design and layout ∼

∼ Suggestions for future titles ∼

∼ Any other comments you may have ∼

There's More at StopStartBooks.com!
At StopStartBooks.com you can discover great new
products for yourself, family and friends.